Learn by Example: JavaScript for Front-End and Mobile App Development
By
Damien M. O'Halloran

ABOUT THIS BOOK

Audience

This book is designed for people that are new to coding to take them from beginner to an accomplished level wherein the reader can understand advanced concepts in HTML, CSS, and JavaScript and put these together to code and launch their own front-end sites and mobile applications. The book is divided into sections on HTML, CSS, JavaScript, and mobile app development using Apache Cordova. Each section starts by providing the basic understanding of code syntax and logic and then dives into advanced topics in each section to help the reader develop a deep understanding of the underlying model.

Prerequisites

No prior knowledge of coding is assumed for the reader. However, this does not mean that this book is only introductory. This book starts with the basics and slowly builds upon this foundation to introduce advanced topics. Assignments throughout each section are designed to challenge the reader to critically think about concepts and convert this conceptual framework into a practical example. By successfully completing the assignments, the reader can move to a more advanced level.

Copyright and Disclaimer

Table of Contents

5

PART 1: INTRODUCTION TO HTML

What is HTML?

Hypertext Markup Language (HTML) is a markup language that is used to create web pages. A markup language is designed to order the presentation or type of text, and typically contains features or elements called *tags* that define specific presentation styles. HTML functions alongside Cascading Style Sheets (CSS) as well as JavaScript, and together these three languages form the basis for much of the internet. Web browsers contain parsers that can interpret HTML, and contain compilers that can interpret and compile the corresponding JavaScript. As well as parsers and compilers, web browsers also come with specific rendering engines that enable the correct presentation, or rendering, of HTML documents. So in essence, HTML is a basic markup language that contains the building blocks of a dynamic, interactive webpage, and browsers contain the parser and rendering engines that interpret and organize the underlying code into a visual layout. The main HTML markup features are elements, which are declared by tags, written using angle brackets. Tags such as <img > and <input > directly introduce specific types of content onto the page. Other tags such as <p> or <div> surround text and provide information about its organization, and may include other tags as sub-elements. The browser rendering engine will never render these tags specifically on a page but rather use them to interpret and parse the content of the page.

Sending and Receiving HTML

The Web is composed of HTML documents (and some other document types and data) transmitted from servers to browsers using the Hypertext Transfer Protocol (HTTP). HTTP functions as client-server model that is based on a request from the client and a response form the server. For example, a browser might be a client and an application running on a computer that hosts a website or program may be the server. Therefore, the client submits an HTTP request to the server; this request may be a form that a user filled out on a website and then clicked submit. The server will return a response to the client. The response contains a completion status (referred to as the HTTP 200 OK status) about the request and may include requested content in the message body. HTTP can return and serve different types of data in addition to text, for example, images, audio, or videos. In order for the browser to interpret what kind of data it will receive the server will send meta data associated with the request that describe the attributes like the character encoding and also the data type e.g. UFT-8 encoding and text/html document type.

The Document Object Model

The Document Object Model (DOM) is a programming interface for HTML and Extensible Markup Language (XML) documents. It represents the page so that programs can change the document structure, style, and content. The DOM represents the document as nodes and objects. That way, programming languages can connect to the page at specific hooks. Scripting languages such as JavaScript can modify how the DOM is represented.

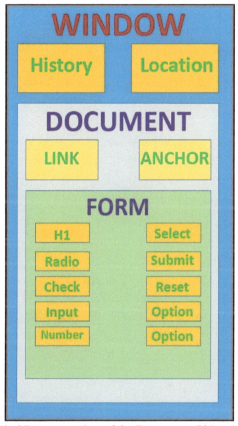

Figure 1. Graphical Representation of the Document Object Model (DOM).

Code editors to write HTML

Web pages can be created and modified by using a text editor. Often the choice of which editor to use can come down to personal preference. However, a very popular choice with nice functionality is Sublime Text - https://www.sublimetext.com/ - that is a proprietary cross-platform source code editor with a Python application-programming interface (API). It natively supports many programming languages and markup languages, and functions can be added with plugins. Another very popular code editor is Brackets - http://brackets.io/ - which is an open-source editor written in HTML, CSS, and JavaScript with a primary focus on web development. It was created by Adobe Systems and is currently maintained on GitHub by Adobe and other open-sourced developers. Brackets is available for cross-platform download on Mac, Windows, and is compatible with most Linux distributions. A nice feature of brackets is its live preview feature for HTML, CSS and JavaScript editing functionality. When one clicks on the respective code snippet in CSS/HTML the web browser immediately shows the output relating to that code snippet in the web browser. This creates a convenient way to see how edits to code can alter the webpage in a browser. For a more comprehensive list of HTML editors, you can visit this page: https://en.wikipedia.org/wiki/List_of_HTML_editors

HTML tags

HTML tags normally come in pairs like <p> and </p> with the first tag in a pair called the opening tag, the second tag called the closing tag. The closing tag is written like the opening tag, but with a forward slash inserted before the tag name e.g. </p>. HTML tags are case-insensitive.

The conventional "Hello World" example

All HTML documents must start with a document type declaration: <!DOCTYPE html>. The HTML document itself begins with <html> and ends with </html>. The visible part of the HTML document is between <body> and </body>. In the following example, the term Hello World will be printed to the browser screen:
This is the HTML code:

```
<!DOCTYPE html>
<head>
</head>
<body>
    <h1>Hello World</h1>
</body>
</html>
```

This will be seen in the browser when we open the HTML document containing the HTML code above in a browser:

Hello World

In this example above, "Hello World" can be seen in the browser by using header tags. HTML headers are defined with the <h1> to <h6> tags, with <h1> being the largest size.

Common HTML tags and their functions

Later in this book, we will highlight specific HTML tags that are commonly used in web development for different tasks, but for now, we will provide a reference list of HTML tags:

<!-->	This tag, is the comments tag which is used to hide comments within your HTML code
<!DOCTYPE>	This is the document type tag that is a declaration that lets the browser know what type of document to expect. The document type tag does not have an end tag.
<a>	The anchor tag connects two pages with the help of an address. The link forms the attribute of the tag and needs to be inserted inside the opening <a> tag. The link attribute is defined using href which makes the link clickable
<address>	The address tag defines the contact information of the owner or author of the page
<area>	The area tag is used to define the area of a clickable section when using area mapping.
<article>	This tag is used to represent a component of a page that consists of a self-contained composition in a document or a page of the site.
<aside>	The aside tag isolates a segment of the substance from the fundamental substance of the page. Utilizing this label moves the concentration from the fundamental segment of the page to feature extra data
<audio>	The audio tag allows music, or any other type of sound file, to be embedded in the webpage. Audio tags are used so that files embedded in these tags can be listened to directly in the browser rather than downloading the file to listen to it.
<b>	The bold tag is used to make text bold, or stand out from other text on a webpage.
<base>	The base element allows authors to specify the document base URL for the purposes of structuring other URLs
<blockquote>	This tag is used to specify a section that is quoted from another source.

<body>	The body tag displays all the content of an HTML document, such as text, hyperlinks, images, tables, lists, etc.
 	This tag will let you add a line break to the text. It puts anything that comes after it on a new line.
<button>	The button tag defines a clickable button.
<canvas>	The canvas tag is a blank area on the page which is used to draw graphics
<caption>	The caption tag is used to insert a title for a table and is inserted directly after the table tag.
<cite>	The cite tag defines the title of a work, e.g., an article
<code>	The code tag is used to define a reference or piece of code embedded on a page. However, using CSS might help the author enhance the piece of text more efficiently.
<col>	The column tag specifies styles for the cells of the table within a colgroup tag. The column tag is used to apply styles to entire columns, instead of repeating the styles for each cell, for each row.
<colgroup>	The colgroup tag specifies styles for the columns in a table for formatting. Specifies a group of one or more columns in a table for formatting.
<datalist>	The datalist tag specifies a list of pre-defined options for an input element. Using autocomplete feature, it hints to the user the values in the drop down.
<div>	The div tag defines a division or a section in an HTML document.
<em>	The <em> HTML tag is a phrase tag. It renders emphasized text. Similar to the italics tag.
<embed>	The embed tag is similar to the applet tag, which allows a third party plugin to be inserted into a page. This external plugin adds application or interactive content onto a page.
<fieldset>	The HTML <fieldset> element can be used to group several elements within a web form.
<figcaption>	The figcaption tag defines a caption for a figure element. Similar to the caption tag for a table. It does not have any alignment property.
<figure>	The HTML <figure> element is self-contained content
<footer>	The footer tag defines a footer for a document or section.

`<form>`	The form tag is one of the most important aspects of interactive pages. It can be used to create an HTML form for user input.
`<head>`	The head tag is mainly responsible for the functioning of the body. The head tag includes all the script and style elements, and must include a title for the document
`<header>`	The header tag specifies a header for a document or section. The header element should be used as a container for introductory content or a set of navigational links.
`<h1> to <h6>`	The `<h1>` to `<h6>` tag elements represent the six sizes of headings whereby `<h1>` is the biggest section and `<h6>` is the smallest.
`<hr>`	The HTML `<hr>` element represents a break between paragraph-level elements
`<html>`	The HTML tag tells the browser that this is an HTML document. This tag is the container for all other HTML elements (except for the `<!DOCTYPE>` tag).
`<i>`	The italic tag is used to highlight important words or sentences within text. Similar to the Italic text found in most word processing programs.
`<iframe>`	The HTML Inline Frame element (`<iframe>`) effectively embeds another HTML page into the current page.
`<img>`	This tag defines images in an HTML document. A source and an alt are mandatory attributes of this tag. Technically, they are not inserted; they are the source of the image linked to the tag.
`<input>`	Using the `<input>` HTML tag an author can accept inputs from users making a page interactive. It is used within the form tag. We will use this tag extensively throughout this book.
`<kbd>`	This tag defines keyboard input. The font style in this tag is different from normal text.
`<label>`	The label element does not render anything special for the user. However, it provides a usability improvement for mouse users, because if the user clicks on the text within the label element, the cursor focus is shifted to the relative input element. For this functionality the "for" attribute is used on label.
`<legend>`	The legend tag defines a caption for the fieldset

	element. It is similar to the caption tag for a table. It does not have any alignment properties.
<li>	The <li> element can be used to define a specific item within a list. The <li> element must be contained inside a parent element that is declared using the <ol> tag for ordered lists or the <ul> tag for unordered lists.
<link>	The <link> tag creates a link with an external source.
<main>	The HTML <main> element is used to refer to the main content of the <body> of a document.
<map>	The map tag is used to define a client-side image-map, wherein an author can make a part of image clickable.
<meta>	The meta tag provides metadata about the HTML document. Metadata will not be rendered on the website by the browser
<meter>	The meter tag defines a scalar measurement within a known range, or a fractional value.
<nav>	The nav tag defines the navigation links of the page.
<noscript>	The noscript tag defines an alternate content for users that have disabled scripts in their browser or have a browser that does not support script.
<object>	The object tag adds external elements to pages, just by linking the source. External elements can be animated flash, webpages, applets, PDFs, etc. It is placed within the body tag only.
<ol>	Ordered list lets the user have a list of elements with a numbered or alphabetical bulleted list.
<optgroup>	The optgroup tag helps you create sections or groups within a drop-down list.
<option>	This tag creates the items for selection in the drop-down list, i.e., options to be selected from the select tag.
<p>	The p tag defines a paragraph on the page
<param>	The param tag is used to define parameters for plugins embedded with an object element.
<pre>	This tag lets you use preformatted text, where the user can define or print text on page 'as is' written inside the tag. Whitespace inside this element is displayed exactly as written.
<progress>	The progress tag represents the progress of a task.
<q>	The q tag defines a short inline quotation.
<s>	The s tag defines the encompassed text is not more

	accurate or correct. Should not be used to define replaced or deleted text.
<samp>	The samp tag is a phrase tag. It defines sample output from a computer program.
<script>	The script tag enables the author to insert scripting language into document, such as JavaScript. This tag lets you validate, manipulate, and affect content dynamically.
<section>	The section tag defines a section of the page, such as chapters, headers, footers, etc.
<select>	The select tag lets the author define a drop down of options to select from, which are hardcoded in HTML. A list of items are inserted using the option tag within the select tag.
<small>	This tag reduces size of the text from the normal size to a smaller size.
<source>	The source tag is nested within the audio and video tag, letting it define the source of the media to be used by the browser, based on its media type or codec support.
<span>	The span tag is used to add custom styling to inline elements. There are no self-properties defined for this tag.
<strong>	The strong tag is a phrase tag. It defines important text.
<style>	The style tag is used to define styling for the page and elements on the page.
<sub>	The <sub> HTML tag is used to define subscript subscript tag is used to define or format text, by shifting the text to the lower part of the current line, called the baseline. This tag is usually used when expressing scientific formulae.
<sup>	The <sup> HTML tag is used to define superscript text e.g. in a Math formula
<table>	The <table> HTML tag is used to present data in a tabular format. The <tr> HTML tag is used to insert rows, while the <td> HTML tag is used to insert columns. The table header is defined using the <th> HTML.
<tbody>	The <tbody> HTML tag, is the table body tag and is used to group the body content in an HTML table.
<td>	The <td> tag is an individual cell in table, it helps form the columns of the table. An HTML table has

	two kinds of cells:
<textarea>	The <textarea> tag defines multi-line text input. The size of a text area can be specified by the columns and rows attribute inline or externally using CSS
<tfoot>	The <tfoot> tag is used to define a set of rows summarizing the columns of the table
<th>	The <th> tag defines a header for a cell in a table.
<thead>	The <thead> tag is used to group the header content in a table.
<time>	The <time> tag is used to define a time period. It will often include the datetime attribute and contains a closing </time> tag.
<title>	The <title> tag defines the title of the page. This tag is placed inside the header section of a HTML document:
<tr>	The <tr> HTML tag defines a row in an HTML table. It contains the <td> HTML or <th> HTML tags, which define the visual columns of the table.
<ul>	Unordered list HTML tag lets the user create a list of elements without numbers or alphabetical bulleted list. Each item in the list will be depicted alongside a black bullet point (•).
<var>	The var tag is a phrase tag. It defines a variable. Similar to the italics tag.
<video>	The <video> tag is a media tag that defines a section containing a video in a website or page. Can be used with the source attribute src="myURL" to identify the external source and the dimensions of the video frame can also be defined using the width attribute e.g., width="500"

Elements and Attributes

In most cases, an HTML element usually consists of an opening tag and a closing tag, with specific content inserted in between. It is important to note that the HTML element is everything from the opening tag to the closing tag. So in the example below the element is everything from the opening <p> tag to the closing </p> tag and the text in between which reads "Your Awesome Code…":

```
<p>Your Awesome Code...</p>
```

HTML elements can also contain attributes that can provide additional information about an element. When adding an attribute to an element, it always needs to be declared in the opening tag and not the closing tag. The syntax for an attribute usually come as a name value pair e.g., name=SomeValue. For example, HTML links are defined within the <a> tag by declaring the link with a href as follows:

```
<a href="https://www.bbc.com">This is a link to the BBC</a>
```

Another example is the style attribute. The style attribute can be used to specify the styling of an element, like color, font, size etc. In the following example, we are styling the color of the text containing within a <p> element:

```
<p style="color:blue">Your Awesome Code...</p>
```

Good code is commented code

You can add comments to your HTML source code by using the following syntax:

```
<!-- This is a comment -->

<p>Your Awesome Code...</p>

<!-- Remember to add more awesome code here -->
```

Notice that there is an exclamation point (!) in the opening tag, but not in the closing tag. It is very important to comment your code, so that you (and others) can follow the logic in your code and fix bugs or reproduce the effect of some code. This is not just true for writing HTML, but any code, and later in this book, we will discuss commenting CSS and JavaScript. The importance of commenting code cannot be stressed enough, and will save you a lot of headache when you try to re-write code or share code with another person

Assignment 1.1

Download one of the text editors that we discussed in this chapter and open a new blank document. Save this document with the file extension .html. You can call this document whatever you want. In this document, put together a basic HTML page with all the required tags that are needed in a HTML page.

In addition to a writing a basic HTML document, include the following elements and attributes:
1. Two separate links to different webpages
2. A title
3. Headings using at least three different header tags with different color fonts for each
4. And finally, be sure to include examples of single line and multi-line commenting in your code.

After writing your HTML code, save your .html file and then open it in your browser, to ensure all the features that you coded work correctly.

Unordered lists

Listing items on a webpage is a very common task; in fact, it is so common, there are specific HTML tags to help you out. Lists are used to group together related pieces of information so they can be visually associated with each other. In addition to the visual aspects, they are very convenient structurally. For example, they can be assigned a specific class and then styled in a certain manner or modified based on user behavior, e.g. a click. Lists can be ordered or unordered. An unordered list starts with the <ul> HTML tag. Each list item starts with the <li> tag as follows:

```
<ul>
  <li>Math</li>
  <li>Chem</li>
  <li>Bio</li>
</ul>
```

In the case of unordered lists, the list items will be marked with bullets (small black circles) by default. This list above will be seen in the browser as follows:

- Math
- Chem
- Bio

Ordered lists

An ordered list starts with the <ol> tag. Again, each list item starts with the <li> HTML tag. For an ordered list, the list items will be marked with numbers by default:

```
<ol>
  <li>Math</li>
  <li>Chem</li>
  <li>Bio</li>
</ol>
```

This ordered list will be seen in the browser as shown below. Note the numbering of each list entry instead of the bullet points:

1. Math
2. Chem
3. Bio

HTML forms

HTML forms are another very common feature of websites. HTML Forms are used when you want to collect some data from the user. For example, during a registration process you might like to collect information such as name, date of birth, location, email address etc. A form will take input from the site visitor and then post it to a server-side application such as a PHP script. The back-end, or server-side, application will perform required processing on the transferred data. There are various form elements available like text fields, textarea fields, drop-down menus, radio buttons, checkboxes, etc. The HTML <form> tag is used to create an HTML form and a closing </form> ends the form. A basic form has the following syntax

```
<form action="/some_server_script.php">
    User First name:<br>
    <input type="text" name="firstname" value="John"><br>
    User Last name:<br>
    <input type="text" name="lastname" value="Doe"><br><br>
    <input type="submit" value="Submit">
</form>
```

The code above will generate a form that will be seen in the browser as follows:

User First name:

John

User Last name:

Doe

Submit

Viewport

The visible part of a web page is referred to as the Viewport, and so naturally the dimensions of the Viewport will change significantly on different types of devices. If we are only designing applications for computer browsers, then the Viewport will have a consistent size but once we start viewing HTML documents on tablets, and mobile devices we need to scale the Viewport to make the HTML content readable, and this is achieved using the Viewport <meta> HTML tag. The <meta> HTML tag is not rendered in the browser but instead provides the browser with instructions on how to control the web page dimensions to ensure proper scaling of the content. Inside the <meta> tag, we can provide a name, which should be equal to viewport as shown below. Next, we can use the content attribute to set the width of the viewport to the width of the viewing device, and finally we define how the content will be scaled when the content is first loaded in the browser – this is usually set to 1.0. The syntax of the <meta> tag is as follows:

```
<meta name="viewport" content="width=device-width, initial-scale=1.0">
```

It is worth pointing out that, depending on the HTML document content, this approach may not render your site exactly as you would like, but it should help make it look better on smaller devices. To provide a more custom fit, we will style individual elements and sections using Cascading Style Sheet Media queries later in this book.

Assignment 1.2

In the previous assignment, you generated a basic HTML document. Now add two lists to that document. One list should be unordered and the other list should be ordered.

Next, add a table with three table headers and two table row entries per heading (*hint*: refer to the table of HTML tags earlier in this section to identify the correct table tags).

Finally, write the HTML code to render the following web form (shown below) in the browser. (*hint*: use the <input type="value"> tag and attribute to add a checkbox, radio buttons, or password fields. In each case, the value just needs to be set to "checkbox", "password", or "radio").

First Name: Jane

Last Name: Doe

Password ••••••••

Age: over 30

Gender: ○Male ○Female

State: ☐DC ☐VA

submit form   reset form

PART 2: INTRODUCTION TO CSS

What is CSS?

Cascading Style Sheets (CSS) is an expressive styling language used to describe the presentation of a webpage. CSS provides a set of instructions about how different elements (like for example, the HTML tags discussed in the last section) are to be rendered on the webpage. CSS can also be used to style these elements by color, font type etc. Rather than defining styles in every HTML page, with CSS we can define styles once for multiple HTML pages by referencing an external CSS file from within each HTML document.

CSS Versions

CSS versions are organized into various levels and profiles where each level of CSS provides new features that build upon older profiles or levels. The CSS profiles are made up of different levels of CSS that are built for a particular device or browser. The first CSS official specification was published in 1996 by Håkon Wium Lie and Bert Bos. The next level of CSS specifications (level 2) were developed by the World Wide Web Consortium and published in 1998. In levels 3 of CSS, which were first published in 1999; it became divided into several separate documents called modules with each module contributing new features that were defined in the level 2 of CSS.

The Problem Solved by CSS

The goal of HTML was to provide a language that the browser could interpret and render to represent specific content. However, when the ability to style individual HTML elements using tags like <font> was introduced in the HTML 3.2 specification of HTML, it became possible to style HTML elements however we wanted. This offered a way to enhance the user interface and make a web site more visually pleasing, but at the same time, it made the job of developers very tedious as it meant that each individual tag needed to be styled in a specific way based on fonts or colors. To get around this problem, Cascading Style Sheets were introduced. With CSS, developers were able to bundle all of the styling for an HTML page or series of HTML pages, into a single document (CSS file), and for each HTML page the developer could reference the external CSS file in order to style specific elements on that page. Now with a single CSS file, developers can control the look and feel or any number of HTML documents without having to add any styling to the individual HTML tags. This is the crux of the problem that was solved by CSS and it is important to note for a few reasons. Firstly, it is always good to learn about the history of the internet and the languages of the browser, and secondly by defining the problem solved with CSS it serves as a lesson to new developers. This lesson is that the most effective way to style anything within an HTML document should always be via the CSS file, and whenever you are styling individual tags on an HTML document, you are not really using CSS effectively nor using it the way that it was actually intended to be used.

CSS Syntax

A CSS rule-set consists of a selector and a declaration block. Selectors point to HTML elements, which you want to style. Declarations contain one or more instructions separated by semicolons. Each declaration will include a CSS property name and its corresponding value, separated by a colon. A CSS declaration must always be surrounded by curly braces, and end with a semi-colon:

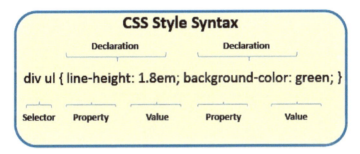

Figure 2. CSS style syntax depicting a selector and two declaration blocks. Each declaration is composed of a property and a value

In the following example, all <p> elements will be center-aligned, with a blue text color:

```
p {
color: blue;
text-align: center;
}
```

CSS selectors can be used to select HTML elements based on their element name, id, class, attribute etc. The above code will select all <p> tags on a page but ignore other elements. The id selector uses the id attribute of an HTML tag to select a specific element. The id of an element should be unique within a page, so the id selector is used to select only one unique element. To select an element with a specific id, write the hash # character, followed immediately by the id of the element. Below, the style rule will be applied only to the HTML element with id="sectionA":

```
#sectionA {
text-align: center;
color: red;
}
```

The corresponding HTML that contains the paragraph <p> tag that has an attribute id set to sectionA, may be as follows:

```
<p id="sectionA">Your awesome code</p>
<p>This paragraph does not have the same id and therefore is not affected by the style</p>
```

The class selector can also select HTML elements with a specific class attribute. To select elements of a specific class, you can write a period character immediately before the name of the class. In the example below, all HTML elements that are defined by the class="middle" will be green and center-aligned:

```
.middle {
text-align: center;
color: green;
}
```

The corresponding HTML that contains both a <h1> tag and also a <p> tag set to the class of "middle" may be as follows:

```
<h1 class="middle">Green and center-aligned heading</h1>
<p class="middle">Green and center-aligned paragraph</p>
```

If you want a specific tag and a class to be styled in the same way, you can group these selectors together to minimize writing code. To group selectors, separate each selector with a comma. In the example below, we have grouped the selectors from the code above i.e. <p> tags, #sectionA id tag, and tags where the class is set to middle:

```css
p, .middle, #sectionA {
color: blue;
text-align: center;
}
```

Commenting CSS

As discussed in the first section, commenting code is imperative for good coding practice, not just for seasoned programmers but also for beginners. Comments are used to explain the code and may help when you edit the source code at a later date. Comments are ignored by browsers. A CSS comment starts with /* and ends with */. Comments can also span multiple lines as follows:

```css
h1 {
color: blue;
/* single-line comment */
text-align: center;
}

/* multi-line
comment */
```

How to insert CSS

External: CSS stylings can be accessed through an external file. With an external style sheet, you can change the look of an entire website by changing just one file as follows:

```html
<head>
    <link rel="stylesheet" type="text/css" href="myAwesomeStyles.css">
</head>
```

Note the <link> tag which contains a definition of what you are linking to i.e. stylesheet and its type i.e. text/css, followed by the relative path (or in some cases may actually be a URL) to the external CSS file. An external style must be saved with a .css extension.

Internal: An internal style sheet may be used if one single page has a unique style. Internal styles are defined within <style> element tags inside the <head> section of an HTML page. In the following example, we group two CSS sets within the <style> tags, which will sit inside the <head> tags of the HTML document. Note that the <style> tag has an opening and also a closing tag </style> as follows:

```
<style>
p, .middle, #sectionA {
color: blue;
text-align: center;
}

h1 {
color: blue;
/* single-line comment */
text-align: center;
}
/* multi-line
comment */
</style>
```

Inline: An inline style may be used to apply a very specific style to a single HTML element. To use inline styles you can add the style attribute to the appropriate element. The style attribute can contain any CSS property. In the example below, we show how to change the color of a <h1> element text as follows:

```
<!DOCTYPE html>
<html>
    <body>
        <h1 style="color:green;">Hello World</h1>
        <p>This is a paragraph.</p>
    </body>
</html>
```

An interesting side effect of being able to define the styles at different levels, is that you may have the same style defined in more than one place (this can happen especially when using external frameworks). If there are multiple styles declared for an element, they will cascade based on the following priority: 1) Inline style (inside an HTML element) and 2) External and Internal style sheets (in the head section). Therefore, an inline style (inside a specific HTML element) has the highest priority, which means that it will override a style defined inside the <head> tag or in an external style sheet

CSS Selectors

As mentioned above, there are multiple ways to select HTML elements, and below is a list of commonly used CSS selectors.

.hello	Selects all elements with class="hello"
#myAge	Selects the element with id="myAge"
*	Selects all elements
p	Selects all <p> elements
div, p	Selects all <div> elements and all <p> elements
div p	Selects all <p> elements inside <div> elements
div > p	Selects all <p> elements where the parent is a <div> element
div + p	Selects all <p> elements that are placed immediately after <div> elements
p ~ ul	Selects every <ul> element that is preceded by a <p> element
[title~=biology]	Select all elements with a title attribute containing the word "biology"

[lang|=sp]	Selects all elements with a language attribute value starting with "sp"
a[href^="https"]	Selects every <a> element where the href attribute value begins with "https"
a[href$=".pdf"]	Selects every <a> element where the href attribute value ends with ".pdf"
a:active	Selects the active link
p::after	Insert something after content of each <p> element
p::before	Insert something before the content of each <p> element
input:checked	Selects every checked <input> element
input:disabled	Selects every disabled <input> element
input:enabled	Selects every enabled <input> element
p:first-child	Selects every <p> element that is the first child of its parent
p:first-of-type	Selects every <p> element that is the first <p> element of its parent
p:last-child	Selects every <p> element that is the last child of its parent
p:last-of-type	Selects every <p> element that is the last <p> element of its parent
input:focus	Selects the input element which has focus
a:hover	Selects links on

	mouse over
input:in-range	Selects input elements with a value in a specified range
:not(p)	Selects every element that is not a <p> element
p:nth-child(2)	Selects every <p> element that is the second child of its parent
p:nth-last-child(2)	Selects every <p> element that is the second child of its parent, counting from the last child
p:nth-last-of-type(2)	Selects every <p> element that is the second <p> element of its parent, counting from the last child
p:nth-of-type(2)	Selects every <p> element that is the second <p> element of its parent

Assignment 2.1

Generate a simple html page that contains multiple headings and some random text inside <p> tags (*hint*: a great place to generate random text is at this site: https://www.lipsum.com/).

Next, using external style sheets set the color and alignment of the headings and paragraphs using id selectors, class selectors, and tag selectors.

Next, add external styling that will change the color of one of the headings after the user hovers over the heading text (*hint*: refer to the CSS selectors table above to find the right selector).

Background and colors

Font colors and element backgrounds can be altered by using the color and background-color properties. The syntax to style text and background color for headings that use the <h1> tag and <p> tag elements would be as follows:

```
h1{
background-color: green;
color: blue;
}
p{
background-color: yellow;
color: blue;
}
```

The styling above would be rendered as follows in the browser. The upper element is defined using <h1> tags and the bottom element is defined by <p> tags:

Green and center-aligned heading

Green and center-aligned paragraph

It is also possible to set the background to an image as follows:

```
body {
background-image: url("some_image.jpg");
}
```

The relative path of the image can be supplied between double quotation marks. Color can also be defined using Red Green Blue (RGB) values as follows:

```
#sectionA {
background-color:rgb(255,0,0);
opacity:0.6;
}
```

The transparency of the element can also be defined using the opacity property (from 0.0 – 1.0). The styling above will be seen in the browser as follows:

Your awesome code

Therefore, in addition to declaring the color type, it is also possible to specify the color using a hexadecimal (HEX) value in the form: #rrggbb. The rr (red), gg (green) and bb (blue) are hexadecimal values between 00 and ff. For example, #ff0000 is displayed as red, because red is set to its highest value (ff) while the other values are set to the lowest value (00). Similarly #0000ff would be blue as only blue is specified and is given the maximum value i.e. ff. For example, the main Facebook Blue color is #3B5998 in Hex, and rgb(59, 89, 152) in RGB. A nice place to find the RGB or HEX colors that you might want is at the following sites:

- https://www.w3schools.com/colors/colors_picker.asp
- https://www.rapidtables.com/web/color/RGB_Color.html
- https://htmlcolorcodes.com/color-picker/

Borders, margins, and padding

To style a border around an element, you can use the border property. The border property accepts multiple values that specify aspects of the border, such as the width, thickness, or color. The main border property values are shown and described in the following table:

border-width	This will specify the width of the border line
\<length\>	This will define the length of the border, and the units can be measured in px units.
\<width\>	This will define the width of the border, and the units can be measured in px units.
\<height\>	This will define the heigth of the border, and the units can be measured in px units.
thin	This is a predefined thickness and is the equivalent of 1px
medium	This is a predefined thickness and is the equivalent of 3px
thick	This is a predefined thickness and is the equivalent of 5px
border-style	This will specify the type of line drawn around the

	element e.g. dotted or ridge	
color	This will specify the color of the border	

Here is an example using the border property to define a solid red border that will be 3px thick. The height and width properties define the dimension of the element that will be have a border:

```
#sectionA {
border: 3px solid red;
height: 200px;
width: 200px;
}
```

The styling above may be seen in the browser as follows:

In the above example, the border-style is supplied as a value to the border property. We could also have defined the solid style by providing it as a value to the border-style property. In fact, if you want to expand the styling of the border above, it would be better practice to define the style as a value on the border-style property as this will open up the option of other values such as ridge, as mentioned in the table above.

Borders are useful to provide a visual frame around an element, but sometimes we may just want to define space for an element without giving it a visual border. The margin properties are used to create space around elements i.e. in relation to other elements. The CSS margin property can be used to define the space on all sides of an element i.e. top, bottom, right, left. The margin feature has separate properties that can define space on any given side. To define space for the top, you can use the margin-top property and provide the space value as px units. Same approach is used to define margin space using the margin-right property, margin-bottom property, or margin-left property. The space defined for each property can also be specified using the auto value, which is calculated by the device or browser. The space can also be defined by providing a percentage (%) value, which is calculated as a percentage of the screen or browser. In the following example, we set different margins for all four sides of a <h1> element, while also providing a border and background color:

```
h1 {
border: 1px solid black;
margin-top: 100px;
margin-bottom: 100px;
margin-right: 150px;
margin-left: 80px;
background-color: lightblue;
}
```

The styling in the above example, may be rendered in the browser as follows (Note how the greater margin-right value, which is defined first, causes the text to be off-center to accommodate a 150px margin):

Green and center-aligned heading

The CSS padding properties are used to generate space around an element's content. While margin create space between elements, padding will create space within an element from its border. Very similar to the syntax for margins, padding can also be defined using properties specific to padding space on all sides of an element's content i.e. padding-top, padding-right, padding-bottom, padding-left. Also similar to margins, the padding properties are supplied values as pixels, and percentages.

In the following example, we define different padding styles for all four sides of a <h1> element using each of the four padding properties and supplying them with specific dimensions using px units:

```
h1 {
padding-top: 50px;
padding-right: 30px;
padding-bottom: 50px;
padding-left: 80px;
}
```

Before the padding style was defined to the <h1> tag element, the content was rendered in the browser as follows:

Green and center-aligned heading

After padding style was defined, it was rendered as follows (Note, the off-center position because of the greater padding-left property value i.e. 80px):

Green and center-aligned heading

Forms

The look of an HTML form can be greatly improved by providing CSS styling. We can use the width property to determine the width of the input field for a form:

```
input {
width: 50%;
}
```

This will be seen in the browser as follows. Notice that the submit button (bottom white rectangle with grey border) is just a long as the text input fields:

User First name:

John

User Last name:

Doe

The example above styles all <input> elements to be 50% width, and this includes the button which is also an <input> type i.e. <input type="button">. This is most likely not the desired effect, and so if we only want to style a specific input type (e.g. text), you can use attribute selectors as follows: input[type=text]. This will only select text fields. We can also select on passwords: input[type=password] or number input types by selecting the input type for numbers: input[type=number]. Not only can we use CSS to select the specific input type, but we can also modify that specific input type's margins, borders, padding etc. This really helps place emphasis on specific parts of the form such as the submit button. In the example below, we style the input text elements to cover the full screen, and use the padding and margin shorthand to specify the top/bottom and left/right paddings and margins only. This is achieved by only supplying two values, which will take the first value and apply it to top and bottom, and the second value and apply to right and left. If you only supply a single value, it will be applied to all four sides; you can specify fields and modify padding, margin, and border for that given field as follows:

```
input[type=text]{
width:100%;
padding:12px 20px;
margin: 8px 0;
}
```

The styling above will be rendered in the browser as follows. Note, how the button is styled different to the input text elements:

User First name:

| John |

User Last name:

| Doe |

Submit

Transitions

When we change a style after a user clicks a button for example, this change will happen straight away; however, sometimes we may want to change the speed by which this occurs. To do this we can use CSS transitions, which provide a way to control animation speed whenever we change styling properties. The transition-property can be used to define the property that will be subjected to a transition change. The transition property may be font-size for example and so the value font-size is supplied to the transition property, but it must also be defined in the code block. For example, below we use the font-size property to set the size font that belongs to a specific id to size 16px. Now we can apply this font-size property to the transition-property and then define the duration and delay that we want to invoke. In the example below we also provide a hover selector to the property font-size with a value of 40px to the element with the id=sample. This will change the font-size when the user hovers over the element:

```
#sample {
font-size: 16px;
transition-property: font-size;
transition-duration: 5s;
transition-delay: 2s;
}
#sample:hover {
font-size: 40px;
}
```

Different browsers have different rendering engines that will organize your HTML, CSS, and JavaScript into a visual representation in the browser. Some of these rendering engines (e.g., webkit) have additional transitions available, whereas some will not be able to render specific transitions. Because of this, it is good practice to check for a specific transition first by using the following code:

```css
@supports (transition: initial) {
/* CSS to use if transitions are supported */
}
```

Buttons

Buttons represent very important design elements. They are often at the end of a form or a call to action. Developers will have many reasons to style buttons, including enhancing usability or to place emphasis. Standard buttons can easily be missed by users because they often look similar to other elements, and therefore styling buttons is a very important part of the user experience. We can style a button as follows:

```css
input[type=button], input[type=submit], input[type=reset] {
background-color: #4CAF50;
border: none;
color: white;
padding: 16px 32px;
text-decoration: none;
margin: 4px 2px;
cursor: pointer;
}
/* Tip: use width: 100% for full-width buttons */
```

This will be seen in the browser as show below:

Assignment 2.2

Design a basic HTML document with several headings and <p> tags. Style the color of the text and backgrounds of each heading and <p> elements differently using both RGB codes and HEX codes by visiting the websites we mentioned earlier in this section.

In Assignment 1.2 you designed a basic HTML form. Now revisit that code and this time divide the input types (i.e. text, password, radio) into separate sections each with their own colored border and specific margins, and padding. Finally, style the submit and reset buttons to be unique to the rest of the form

Navigation bars

Navigation bars can be used to list linked content on a site. Just like the lists that we covered earlier, navigation bars utilize the same <ul> and <li> tags. They are considered unordered, as we do not want to render ordered numbering. We can create a <div> tag with a defined class to contain the navigation bar and then within the <div> we will create an unordered list and style the list properties as follows:

```css
.nav ul {
list-style: none;
background-color: #444;
text-align: center;
padding: 0;
margin: 0;
}
.nav li {
font-family: sans-serif;
font-size: 1.2em;
line-height: 40px;
height: 40px;
border-bottom: 1px solid #888;
}

.nav a {
text-decoration: none;
color: #fff;
display: block;
transition: .3s background-color;
}

.nav a:hover {
background-color: #005f5f;
}
```

The a:hover selector in the style above will change the color of the list item once the mouse hovers over a link. The HTML should be as follows:

```html
<body class="science">
    <header>
        <div class="nav">
            <ul>
                <li class="home"><a href="#">Home</a></li>
                <li class="courses"><a href="#">Courses</a></li>
                <li class="Biology"><a href="#">Biology</a></li>
                <li class="Math"><a href="#">Math</a></li>
                <li class="Physics"><a href="#">Physics</a></li>
            </ul>
        </div>
    </header>
```

The navigation bar coded above may be rendered in the browser as follows. Notice, that the 'Courses' list item is a different color (#005f5f), because that is the item we are hovering over:

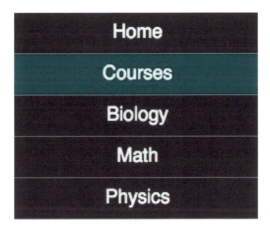

Drop-down menus

In the previous example using navigation bars, we saw how the a:hover selector can change the color of a list item when the user hovers over that item with the mouse. In a similar fashion, we can use the hover selector to only display text upon hover, and using this approach, we can style drop-down menus by initially setting the display property of some content to none and then changing it upon hover. Typically, the drop-down menu is styled using a <span> tag that is wrapped inside a <div> tag. Therefore, in the example below we want to create a drop down menu for news channels, such that when the user hovers over the title that says News Channels a drop down menu of different channels will be displayed. So firstly, we create an outer <div> tag section, which in the example below is defined by the class named theDrop (can be named anything you like). Inside the outer <div> tag we insert a <span> tag with a class defined as dropSpan. Then finally, we have an inner <div> tag that contains three child <a> tags that each contain content, which in this case is a link to BBC, CNN, and ABC news websites. Therefore, the HTML for a drop-down menu is straightforward, the magic really all happens in our CSS styling. This is what our HTML code should look like:

```
<div class="theDrop">
    <span class="dropSpan">News Channels</span>
    <div class="myLinks">
        <a href="https://www.bbc.com/">BBC</a>
        <a href="https://www.cnn.com/">CNN</a>
        <a href="https://abcnews.go.com/">ABC</a>
    </div>
</div>
```

The HTML code above without any CSS styling will work and will display in the browser as follows:

News Channels
BBC CNN ABC

So next, we want to add some CSS to only reveal the News channel links after the user hovers over the <span> element which contains the text, News Channels. First, we can style the <span> element so it does not look so boring by adding a background-color and text color as well as adding some padding and a border and also setting the font-size to 16px. This is shown below in the style for the class defined as dropSpan. Next, we will organize the whole section by organizing the outer <div> into a block by using the display property for the class defined as theDrop and setting it to inline-property. This will change the look of the News Channel links to be a vertical arrangement instead of a horizontal arrangement as shown above in the browser rendering without styling. Next, we will style the individual links, which are grouped into the class defined as myLinks, and also arrange the individual links into a block. We will also add a hover selector to the myLinks class that will change the background color when they are hovered over. Next comes the most important step of the styling: we need to style the outer <div> tag by adding a hover selector that will change the display of the links from none to block i.e. from hidden to visible. The entire styling syntax should look as follows:

```css
.dropSpan {
background-color: #3b5998;
color: #ffffff;
padding: 16px;
font-size: 16px;
border: solid red 1px;
}
.theDrop {
position: relative;
display: inline-block;
}
.myLinks {
display: none;
position: absolute;
background-color: #f7f7f7;
min-width: 200px;
box-shadow: 0px 8px 16px 0px rgba(0,0,0,0.5);
}
.myLinks a {
color: blue;
padding: 10px 20px;
display: block;
}
.myLinks a:hover {background-color: #ffffff}
.theDrop:hover .myLinks {
display: block;
}
```

The code above will all be rendered in the browser as follows once the user hovers over the outer <div> tag:

45

Range sliders

Range sliders are a fun and interactive feature for a site or mobile application. Technically this is not even a CSS feature as it can be rendered by setting the <input> tag type to range to generate a basic slider. For a basic range slider with no CSS styling the HTML code will be as follows:

```
<h1>Range Slider without CSS</h1>
<div class="mySlider">
    <p>Default range slider:</p>
    <input type="range" min="1" max="1000" value="500">
</div>
```

Really, it is only a type of <input> where the type is range, and it will render in the browser as follows:

Range Slider without CSS

Default range slider:

Now we have a default HTML slider that will function just fine but using CSS it can be styled to look more inviting. To do this we are going to use the exact same HTML code as shown above with one minor addition: we will add a class to the <input> tag which we will set as fancySlider. Then we will change the width of the <div> element to 80%, and also change the width, height and background color of the <input> tag, which we set to class fancySlider as follows:

```
.mySlider {
width: 80%;
}
.fancySlider {
width: 80%;
height: 30px;
background: #dfe3ee;
}
```

This fancier slider with some basic CSS stylings will be rendered in the browser as follows:

Range Slider with CSS

Fancy range slider:

Note, that in the example above we added a class value to the <input> tag so that we could style the actual range slider. However, we could have also selected the <input> tag by using the CSS selector for input or alternatively used the CSS selector for input[type=range]. All are good solutions, just depends on what other elements you have on the page.

Media queries

Media queries are a popular technique for delivering a tailored style sheet to different devices. To demonstrate a simple example, we can change the background color to blue on different devices where the screens are less than or equal to 992pixles in width:

```css
/* Set the background color of body to tan */
body {
background-color: tan;
}
/* On screens that are 992px or less, set the background color to blue */
@media screen and (max-width: 992px) {
body {
background-color: blue;
}
}
```

In this example, we use media queries to create a responsive navigation menu, which varies in design on different screen sizes:

```css
/* The navbar container */
.topnav {
overflow: hidden;
background-color: #333;
}
/* Navbar links */
.topnav a {
float: left;
display: block;
color: white;
text-align: center;
padding: 14px 16px;
text-decoration: none;
}
/* On screens that are 600px wide or less,
make the menu links stack on top of each
other instead of next to each other */
@media screen and (max-width: 600px) {
.topnav a {
float: none;
width: 100%;
}
}
```

The HTML code to generate the menu is as follows:

```
<div class="topnav">
    <a href="#">Bio</a>
    <a href="#">Chem</a>
    <a href="#">Pysch</a>
</div>
```

The links will appear as follows on larger screens over 600pixles wide:

The links will appear as follows on smaller screens that are less than 600pixels:

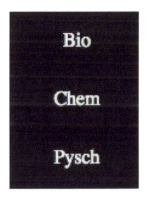

49

Assignment 2.3

Generate a dropdown menu for college course listings that will work on both mobile phones, and on laptop screens. Use Media queries to style the CSS for different device dimensions (*hint:* you can test that your site works well on a mobile phone by going into the developer console and clicking the mobile icon in the bottom right corner as shown below by the red circle).

Figure 3. How to use the mobile viewer from within the developer tools console.

Next, design and style two different range sliders with unique colors, margins, and paddings.

PART 3: INTRODUCTION TO JAVASCRIPT

What is JavaScript?

JavaScript was invented by Brendan Eich, who is the co-founder of the Mozilla project, the Mozilla Foundation, and the Mozilla Corporation. JavaScript is referred to as a dynamic programming language, which means that certain tasks or operations done at compile-time can be done at run-time such as the *eval* function. What this means is that in JavaScript it is possible to change a variable type or modify an object by adding properties such as methods while the program is actually running. When JavaScript is run alongside an HTML document, it can greatly enhance the functionality of the website by increasing dynamic features. JavaScript is a case-sensitive language. This means that language keywords, variables, function names, methods, and other identifiers must always be typed with a consistent case. Some JavaScript objects have the same names as the HTML tags and attributes they represent, and because HTML tags are not case sensitive, you have to pay particular attention to these objects when coding in JavaScript to correctly define their case. A good example of this is the onClick event handler in HMTL, which must be declared as *onclick* in JavaScript code but is commonly defined as *onClick* in HTML.

Where to put JavaScript?

Within an HTML document, JavaScript code can be inserted between <script> tags which have opening and closing tags as follows:

```
<script>

    alert('Hello World');

</script>
```

The above script will generate an alert pop-up in the browser as follows:

You can place any number of scripts in an HTML document. Scripts can be placed in the <body>, or <head> section of an HTML page. External scripts are practical when the same code is used in many different web pages, similar to the utility of external CSS files. External JavaScript files have the file extension .js. To use an external script, put the name of the script file in the source (src) attribute of a <script> opening tag as follows:

```
<script src="myExternalFile.js"></script>
```

External scripts can be referenced with a full URL or with a path relative to the current web page. Placing scripts in external files helps to separate HTML and JavaScript code.

Commenting JavaScript

JavaScript supports two styles of comments. Any text between a // and the end of a line is treated as a single line comment and is ignored by JavaScript. Any text between the characters /* and */ is also treated as a comment; and in this case, these comments may span multiple lines. The following lines of code are examples of single line and multi-line JavaScript comments:

```
// This is a single-line comment

/* This is
a multi-line
comment
*/
```

Reserved Words

A JavaScript identifier must begin with a letter, an underscore (_), or a dollar sign ($). Subsequent characters can be letters, digits, underscores, or dollar signs. Numbers are not allowed as the first character of a variable. In addition to these restrictions, there are also a number of keywords that are reserved and cannot be assigned to a variable. The following are reserved words in JavaScript:

abstract	else	instanceof	super
boolean	enum	int	switch
break	export	interface	synchronized
byte	extends	let	this
case	false	long	throw
catch	final	native	throws
char	finally	new	transient
class	float	null	true
const	for	package	try
continue	function	private	typeof
debugger	goto	protected	var
default	if	public	void
delete	implements	return	volatile
do	import	short	while
double	in	static	with

Optional Semicolons

Like many programming languages, JavaScript uses the semicolon (;) to separate statements from each other. This is important to make the meaning of your code clear: without a separator, the end of one statement might appear to be the beginning of the next, or vice versa. In JavaScript, you can usually omit the semicolon between two statements if those statements are written on separate lines. JavaScript treats a line break as a semicolon if the next non-space character cannot be interpreted as a continuation of the current statement. However, it is best practice to insert semicolons wherever they are necessary, leaving them out can create very difficult to find bugs in your code.

Debugging Tools

In each major browser, a developer tool console can be used for debugging JavaScript code. The console also logs information associated with a web page such as network requests, JavaScript, CSS, security and errors warnings. To print to the console, you can type the following code:

```
console.log("hello world");
```

This will print the string – hello world – to the browser console. To access the console, follow the steps below for each browser:

1. **Chrome**: https://www.google.com/chrome/
2. Open the browser.
3. Click the Tools menu.
4. Click choose developer tools.
5. Click Console.

1. **Firefox**: https://www.mozilla.org/en-US/firefox/new/
2. Open the browser.
3. Open the Tools menu
4. Click the Wed-Developer sub-menu
5. Click the Web-Console option

1. **Safari** https://www.apple.com/safari/
2. Open the Safari browser
3. Click Preferences.
4. Click Advanced.
5. Select "Show Develop menu in menu bar" checkbox.
6. Click Develop menu and then click Choose Show Web Inspector.

The Scope Chain

JavaScript is a lexically scoped language. The scope of a variable is the area in which a specific variable exists. Global variables are defined throughout the code. Local variables are defined in specific code blocks such as functions, which we will cover a little later in this section. Not only do variables exist in specific code blocks, but also each block is actually connected through what is called the Scope Chain. The Scope Chain is actually a set of objects that define the variables within their scope. When the JavaScript compiler is running through a block of code and comes to a variable, it will firstly look at the object in which it currently is sitting to see if it is declared within this object. If it does not find a declaration of this variable within the current object, it will then move to the next object in the scope chain and check to see if it exists there, and it will keep moving through the scope chain until it gets to the global, or outermost, object. If it still cannot find a declaration for that variable, then it will return an error message. The process of searching for a variable declaration is called variable resolution. It is important to understand what happens during variable resolution, as it will help you debug your code when you start seeing Reference Error messages about variables that are not defined.

Let, Const, and Var

Data can be declared and initialized (i.e. assigned a value) using one of three possible definitions – these are Let, Var, or Const. Variables that are declared using var can be accessed inside or outside a scope block, and therefore reassigning a new value to a variable that was defined by var will be modified inside or outside of scope blocks. For example:

```javascript
var myNum = 10;
for (var myNum = 0; myNum < 3; myNum++) {
    console.log(myNum); //0 1 2
}
console.log(myNum); //3
```

However, if we declare the variable myNum using let, it will only be locally scoped:

```javascript
let myNum = 10;
for (let myNum = 0; myNum < 3; myNum++) {
    console.log(myNum); //0 1 2
}.
console.log(myNum); //10
```

56

Therefore, reassigning myNum to another number inside the block scope (i.e. the for loop) will only affect its assignment inside the for loop and not outside. Finally, if we use the const definition to define a variable, we will get an error as follows: TypeError: invalid assignment to const `myNum'. This is because, variables defined using const cannot be changed. However, because let will only scope locally, the following code would not return an error:

```
const myNum = 10;
for (let myNum = 0; myNum < 3; myNum++) {
    console.log(myNum); //0 1 2
}
console.log(myNum); //10
```

You can also combine variable declaration and variable initialization as follows:

```
let a = 0,
    b = 0,
    c = 0;

var d = 0,
    e = 0,
    f = 0;

const g = 0,
      h = 0,
      i = 0;
```

If you don't specify an initial value for a variable with the var or let statements, the variable is declared, but its value is undefined until you assign a value to the variable (i.e. initialize the variable). However, in the case of the const statement, it must be initialized at declaration, see below:

```
let a;
var b;
const c;

console.log(typeof a); //undefined

console.log(typeof b); //undefined

console.log(typeof c); //SyntaxError: missing = in const declaration
```

Data Types

The kinds of values that can be represented and manipulated in a programming language are known as types, and one of the most fundamental characteristics of a programming language is the set of types it supports. In JavaScript, there are six data types:

1. Boolean
2. Number
3. String
4. Undefined
5. Symbol
6. Objects

If you ever want to perform a data type check in JavaScript, you can use the typeof operator to return a string indicating the data type as follows:

```
console.log(typeof 'hello');
// expected output: "string"
```

Boolean

A Boolean value is a binary data type that represent true or false. There are only ever two possible values of this type i.e. true and false. As you might expect, both true and false are reserved keywords in JavaScript because they can be used to evaluate a Boolean expression as follows:

```
Boolean(10 > 9) // returns true
```

Number

Unlike many languages, JavaScript does not make a distinction between integer values and decimal point (floating-point) values. Instead, all numbers in JavaScript are represented as floating-point values, and the job of the developer is often to control how many decimal places he/she wants to see in the Number. This is very different from most other languages, which have separate data types to represent different type of number e.g. integers, or floating-point numbers.

```
var num = 2;
typeof num; // number

var num = -4;
typeof num; // number

var num = 0.6;
typeof num; // number
```

String

A JavaScript string consists of a series of characters like "John Doe". A string can be any text (including a space) inside double or single quotes:

```
var myString = "hello";
```

Undefined

In JavaScript, there is a special data type used to define variables that have not been assigned a value yet, and this is the Undefined data type. If something is undefined it does not mean it does not exist, but rather it just means that it lacks a value assignment. For example:

```
var myValue;

console.log(typeof myValue);
// undefined

myValue = 2;

console.log(typeof myValue);
// number
```

Until a value is assigned to the variable, it will be a typeof undefined, which does not mean it does not exist in memory space, but rather it is awaiting a value to be assigned to it, and until that happens it will be a datatype of undefined.

Symbol

Symbols allow for private properties on objects. We will discuss more about properties on Objects later in this section but for now, we will just demonstrate how a Symbol is declared:

```javascript
var SSN = Symbol("SSN");
var person = { id: '645' };
person[SSN] = "123456";

for (var property in person) {
    if (person.hasOwnProperty(property)) {
        console.log(property); // logs "id", but not "SSN"
    }
}
console.log(person[SSN]); // logs "SSN"
```

Objects

With the exception of the five datatypes we have covered above, everything else in JavaScript belongs to the data type of Object. This includes Functions and Arrays, which we will discuss later in this section. Objects in JavaScript are declared using curly braces and have the following syntax:

```javascript
var person = {}; //Empty Object Declared

person.employee = { name: "Jane Doe" }; // Added a property

console.log(person); //logs the Object person

console.log(person.employee); //logs the Object property

console.log(person.employee.name); //logs the Object property Jane_Doe
```

We can add properties to an object as shown above using Dot Notation. We can also use square brackets i.e. person[employee] = ...
Properties are added as name value pairs using quotes for the value.

Arrays

As we just mentioned, JavaScript arrays are actually object, and are used to store multiple values, similar to a list, but within a single variable. Arrays are defined in JavaScript by listing values e.g. numbers, strings, objects, inside square brackets. It is also fine to declare the elements of an array in JavaScript across multiple lines as shown below:

```javascript
let myArr1 = ['biology', 'chemistry', 'math'];

let myArr2 = ['biology',
              'chemistry',
              'math'
             ];
```

In order to access a specific element within an array, you can refer to each individual element using the index number, which starts at index zero and not 1:

```javascript
console.log(myArr2[0]);//logs biology --> index starts at 0
```

As discussed above, arrays are not unique data types in JavaScript as they are really just Objects. If you use the typeof operator on an array, it will return a type of object data. Because arrays in JavaScript are objects, this means that they can contain all kinds of different data types within a single array, and this can include objects. So yes, arrays are objects and they can contain objects, and in declaring an array in such a manner, you are really creating an object of objects as opposed to an array of objects or an array of arrays, as you might in some other languages. However, the fact that they are objects in JavaScript means that they have a variety of built in properties which can be used to do many things, including examining the contents of the array. For example, the length property will return the number of elements in an array:

```javascript
let myArr2 = ['biology',
              'chemistry',
              'math'
             ];

console.log(myArr2.length);// 3
```

There are also methods on a JavaScript array that can be accessed such as the push() method which adds an element to an array as follows:

```
let myArr2 = ['biology',
              'chemistry',
              'math'
              ];

myArr2.push("physics");

console.log(myArr2[3]);// physics
```

Here is a list of the main methods on arrays in JavaScript:

concat()	Joins two or more arrays, and returns a copy of the joined arrays
copyWithin()	Copies array elements within the array, to and from specified positions
entries()	Returns a key/value pair Array Iteration Object
every()	Checks if every element in an array pass a test
fill()	Fill the elements in an array with a static value
filter()	Creates a new array with every element in an array that pass a test
find()	Returns the value of the first element in an array that pass a test
findIndex()	Returns the index of the first element in an array that pass a test
forEach()	Calls a function for each array element
from()	Creates an array from an object
includes()	Check if an array contains the specified element
indexOf()	Search the array for an element and returns its position
isArray()	Checks whether an object is an array
join()	Joins all elements of an array into a string
keys()	Returns an Array Iteration Object, containing the keys of the original array
lastIndexOf()	Search the array for an element, starting at the end, and returns its position
map()	Creates a new array with the result of calling a function for each array element
pop()	Removes the last element of an array, and returns that element
push()	Adds new elements to the end of an array, and returns the new length
reduce()	Reduce the values of an array to a single value (going

	left-to-right)
reduceRight()	Reduce the values of an array to a single value (going right-to-left)
reverse()	Reverses the order of the elements in an array
shift()	Removes the first element of an array, and returns that element
slice()	Selects a part of an array, and returns the new array
some()	Checks if any of the elements in an array pass a test
sort()	Sorts the elements of an array
splice()	Adds/Removes elements from an array
toString()	Converts an array to a string, and returns the result
unshift()	Adds new elements to the beginning of an array, and returns the new length
valueOf()	Returns the primitive value of an array

The best way to loop through an array in JavaScript is using the forEach method, which executes a function (specifically, a callback function) once for each element present in the array in ascending order. The forEach function can be structured and invoked as follows:

```javascript
let myArr2 = ['biology',
    'chemistry',
    'math'
];


myArr2.forEach(function(item, index, array) {
    console.log(item, index);
});
// biology 0
// chemistry 1
// math 2
```

There are other ways to loop through arrays in JavaScript, which we will cover later in the section entitled Conditions and Loops.

Assignment 3.1

Declare an Array in JavaScript and using the alert function, return that Array's first and last elements.

Make an Array and console.log each element in the array. Then use the push(), pop(), and slice() methods to add a new element onto the array, then remove an element from the array and return a subset of the array. In each case console.log the resulting array to examine the output of each method.

Comparison operators

Comparison operators are used as logic statements to determine equality or difference between variables or values. Given that x = 8, the table below explains the comparison operators:

Operator	Description	Comparing	Returns
==	equal to	x == 4	false
===	equal value and equal type	x === "8"	false
!=	not equal	x != 6	true
!==	not equal value or not equal type	x !== 8	false
>	greater than	x > 9	false
<	less than	x < 12	true
>=	greater than or equal to	x >= 9	false
<=	less than or equal to	x <= 8	true

Of particular note, is the difference between the double equals which compares values, versus the triple equals, which compares values and types. In the second example above, the triple equals returns false because 8 is defined as a Number and not a string, however, the double equals would have returned true in this case, as this does not compare types.

Arithmetic in JavaScript

In JavaScript, you can perform arithmetic using various mathematical operators. These include + for addition, - for subtraction, * for multiplication, / for division, and % for modulo (remainder after division), and ** for exponents. These basic arithmetic operators are described below:

Operator	Description	Example	Result
+	Addition	x = 5 + 2	7
-	Subtraction	x = 5 - 2	3
*	Multiplication	x = 5 * 2	10
/	Division	x = 20 / 2	10
%	Modulus (division remainder)	x = 13 % 2	1
++	Increment	x = 3; ++x	5
--	Decrement	x =3; --x	1
**	Exponentiation	x = 6 ** 4	1296

In addition to these basic arithmetic operators, JavaScript supports more complex mathematical operations through a set of functions as well as constants that are properties on the Math object:

Method	Description
Math.abs(x)	Returns the absolute value of x
Math.acos(x)	Returns the arccosine of x, in radians
Math.asin(x)	Returns the arcsine of x, in radians
Math.atan(x)	Returns the arctangent of a number
Math.atanh(x)	Returns the hyperbolic arctangent of a number
Math.atan2(y, x)	Returns the arctangent of the quotient of its arguments
Math.ceil(x)	Rounds up a floating point value
Math.cos(x)	Returns the cosine of x
Math.exp(x)	Returns the value of Ex
Math.floor(x)	Rounds down a floating point value
Math.log(x)	Returns the natural logarithm (base E) of x
Math.max([x[, y[, ...]]])	Returns the number with the highest value
Math.min([x[, y[, ...]]])	Returns the number with the lowest value
Math.pow(x, y)	Returns the value of x to the power of y
Math.random()	Returns a random number between 0 and 1
Math.round(x)	Rounds to the nearest integer (in the 0.5 will round up)
Math.sin(x)	Returns the sine of x
Math.sqrt(x)	Returns the square root of x
Math.tan(x)	Returns the tangent of an angle

Dates and Times

JavaScript includes a built-in Date() object that is organized as a function constructor to return a representation of time or dates. Date objects also have methods that make it easy to convert times or dates as follows:

```
const now = new Date();

const then = new Date(2010, 0, 1); //The 1st day of the 1st month of 2010

console.log(now); // Date 2018-05-22T19:05:29.405Z

let since = now - then;

console.log(then);//Date 2010-01-01T05:00:00.000Z

console.log(since);//264693961585
```

Assignment 3.2

Use the Date() object in JavaScript to console.log how many days have elapsed since you were born.

hints: you can get the current month as follows:

> Let today = new Date();
> Let nowMonth = today.getMonth();

However, January is 0 and so it is useful to increment nowMonth as follows:

> Let nowMonth = today.getMonth() + 1;

You will also need to remember that JavaScript only has one Number data type, and so you may need to round up or down using the Math Object.

Functions

A JavaScript function is a block of code designed to perform a particular task. A JavaScript function will not do anything until it has been invoked (or called). Function, is another one of JavaScript's reserved keywords and so when naming your function be sure not to name them function (or any other reserved word for that matter). A JavaScript function is defined be declaring the function keyword, followed by a name (optional), followed by parentheses ().The parentheses may include arguments that are passed into the function. The arguments should be separated by commas (parameter1, parameter2 ...). The entire function block is placed inside curly brackets: {}. Function parameters are listed inside the parentheses () in the function definition. Even though the variables may have been passed in from the global object, once these variables are inside a function, they become scoped locally. The syntax for a JavaScript function is as follows:

```
function myFunction(parameter1, parameter2, parameter3) {
code to be executed
}
```

To access the parameters passed into a function, you can use the keyword arguments as follows:

```
function myFunction(a,b,c) {
    console.log("1: " + a + " 2: " + b + " 3: " + c); //1: Jim 2: Ann 3: Brian
    console.log(arguments); //Arguments { 0: "Jim", 1: "Ann", 2: "Brian", … }
}

myFunction("Jim", "Ann", "Brian");
```

Function Invocation

A Function Declaration defines a named function variable without requiring variable assignment. Function Declarations occur as standalone objects and cannot be nested within non-function blocks. Function Declarations must begin with function:

```
function myFunction() {
alert('hello world');
}

myFunction();
```

68

A Function Expression defines a function typically as a variable assignment. Functions defined via Function Expressions can be named or anonymous. Function Expressions can be written with the following syntax:

```
var myFunction = function() {
alert('hello world');
}

myFunction();
```

Functions are first-class objects

Earlier in this section, when we were defining the different data types in JavaScript, we said that apart from the six distinct data types, everything else is an object; well this includes functions. Functions are objects, and because they are objects, they have access to all the other methods and properties that are predefined on all JavaScript objects. As well as being objects, they are also a special type of object called First-Class objects. A first-class object simply means is that you can do everything that you would do with another data types with these first-class objects. Therefore, JavaScript functions inherit from the Object prototype and they can be assigned key value pairs. These pairings are referred to as properties and can themselves be functions, which when on an object are usually called methods. Function objects can also be assigned to variables, they can be passed around as arguments; they can even be assigned as the return values from other functions. Similar to how we used the Dot Notation for objects when we were discussing object data types earlier, we can also apply the dot notation to functions, because they are objects. In fact, we can add properties to functions using dot notations just as we described earlier as follows:

```
function greet() {
    console.log('hello world');
}

greet.alt = "hello earth";//use dot notation to add a property

console.log(greet.alt);//hello earth

greet();//hello world
```

This can be done the exact same way with Function Expression, where a function has been assigned to a variable name as follows:

```
let greet = function(){
    console.log('hello world');
}
greet.alt = "hello earth";
console.log(greet.alt)//hello earth
greet();//hello world
```

Higher order functions

As we just learned, Functions in JavaScript are first-class objects, and this means that just like other first-class objects, functions can actually be passed around just like strings or numbers. In fact, functions can be passed as arguments into other functions. When we pass a function into another function, we create what is called a Higher Order Function or callback. This turns out to be a very useful structure in JavaScript that allows the user to run a function from within another function and only after the outer function has completed. It is very common to use callbacks in JavaScript frameworks like jQuery. We will look at an example demonstrating the syntax involved in a higher-order function (i.e., callback) below:

```
function doMath(number1, number2, callback){
    console.log('Pasing ' + number1 + ' and ' + number2 + ' into the callback');
    callback(number1, number2);
}
//Passing 2 and 4 into the callback

function multiply(x, y){
    let myMult = x * y;
    console.log(x + ' multiplied by ' + y + ' = ' + myMult);
}
//2 multiplied by 4 = 8

function expon(x, y){
    let myExpo = x ** y;
    console.log(x + ' to the power of ' + y + ' = ' + myExpo);
}
//2 multiplied by 4 = 8

doMath(2, 4, multiply);
doMath(2, 4, expon);
```

In this example, we have two callbacks, multiply and expon, and we pass them as arguments into the doMath function to perform basic Math. We could include more callback functions to pass into doMath (e.g., division or square root). Note: we can also write the callback function out during the invocation step, alongside the other two number arguments; you may see callbacks organized that way. See below for example:

```
doMath(2, 4, function expon(x, y) {
    let myExpo = x ** y;
    console.log(x + ' to the power of ' + y + ' = ' + myExpo); //2 to the power of 4 = 16
});
```

Function Hoisting

When the JavaScript compiler starts to run through your code, the first thing it does is to place all declared variables into memory space. However, it does not yet place the value to which a variable has been assigned into memory until later. So if you remember from earlier, when a variable is declared but has not been assigned a value (i.e. not initialized), it is of the type undefined. This is exactly what happens to your code when the compiler first starts to examine your code: it sets all declared variables in memory as undefined. However, functions are not set as undefined unless they are declared as a function expression, and because of this, function declarations are hoisted. However, functions that are assigned to variables (i.e. function expressions) are not hoisted, and will instead be set to undefined. For example in the following code below, we can call the function, greet, before it is declared (because it is hoisted i.e. it is already in memory) but we will get typeof undefined if we console.log a variable prior to initialization. Note that we do not get an error message but rather get typeof undefined when we console.log myNum before we initialize. This is because the variable myNum was already in memory as undefined, and so when we log it prior to initializing it, we get undefined:

```
greet();//hello world (i.e. hoisted)

function greet(){
    console.log('hello world');
}

console.log(myNum);//undefined

var myNum = 6;
```

If we use the definition let to declare myNum we will instead get an error message saying "ReferenceError: can't access lexical declaration`myNum' before initialization" – this is a safer and better way to define variables to avoid problems with hoisting using var. Furthermore, if we declare the function using a function expression instead of a function declaration as above, the function will then be assigned to typeof undef as per var myNum and therefore will be unable to call the function prior to its initialization:

```
greet();//TypeError: greet is not a function

var greet = function () {
    console.log('hello world');
}


greet2();    /*can't access lexical declaration
             `greet' before initialization*/


let greet2 = function () {
    console.log('hello world');
}
```

Immediately Invoked Function Expressions (IIFEs)

An IIFE is an anonymous function contained within a pair of parenthesis and is invoked immediately. The pair of parenthesis creates a local scope for all the code inside of it and makes the anonymous function a function expression. This justifies the name Immediately Invoked Function Expression. It is not called from anywhere else (hence why it's anonymous) but runs just after being created. IIFEs can be used to guard against unintended effects of hoisting and to protect against variable name collision. Arguments can be passed just like any other function:

```
let planet = "earth";
(function (x) {
    console.log('hello planet ' + x); //hello planet earth
}(planet));
```

Note: IIFEs can also be invoked outside the parenthesis but either way is fine.

A major advantage of using IIFEs is to produce safe code that does not collide with the name space in other parts of your code. For example, initialization of a variable inside an IIFE will not cause collision with a variable outside the IIFE:

```
let planet = "earth";

(function () {
    let planet = "mars";
    console.log('hello planet ' + planet); //hello planet mars
}());

console.log('hello planet ' + planet); //hello planet earth
```

This can become very important when loading other frameworks or libraries to ensure that your code does not collide with another person's code.

Methods

JavaScript methods are actions that can be performed on objects. A JavaScript method is a property containing a function definition. Because Functions are first-class objects, it is not surprising that they can contain properties and functions themselves. Functions contained within an Object are referred to as that object's methods. Just like how we access properties on objects using the dot notation, we can also access and invoke methods on objects using dot notation:

```
let myObj = {
    fname: "Jim",
    lname: "Jones",
    full: function(){
        console.log("this is a method!");
    }
}

console.log(myObj.fname); //Jim
console.log(myObj.lname); //Jones
myObj.full(); //this is a method!
```

We can also add methods to objects using dot notation as follows:

```
myObj.newMethod = function(){
    console.log('this is a new method!');
}

myObj.newMethod();//this is a new method!
```

new and *this*

In JavaScript, it is important to be able to keep track of which object a piece of code belongs to, and to facilitate this, JavaScript has the *this* keyword which is a property of every object. The value of this, when used in an object, is the object itself. When we create a new object, the value of this will become the new object when a new object is created. In JavaScript, all function are objects, and therefore have properties, and like other objects will also have its own *this* property when it is invoked. When we invoke a function, it gets a *this* property and we can use the *this* property to access other properties on the function object. This can be very useful, especially when we do not know the name of the function or if it is anonymous and therefore has no name, then we can use the dot notation. In the following code, you can see how *this* is used to access properties within the current object whereas outside of this object, *this* refers to the global object, which in the browser is the window:

```
let myObj = {
    fname: "Jim",
    lname: "Jones",
    full: function(){
        console.log(this);//Object i.e. myObj
        return(this.fname + ' ' + this.lname);
    }
}

console.log(myObj.full()); //Jim Jones

console.log(this);//Window i.e. global object
```

In this example, we create an object with a method called full. From within the full method we can access the properties on the object to which full belongs just by using the *this* keyword.

The way to create an object type, is to use an object constructor function. Objects of the same type can be created on the fly by calling the constructor function with the *new* keyword as follows:

74

```
function myObj(first, last) {
    this.fname = first;
    this.lname = last;
    console.log('This is an object for ' + this.fname + ' ' + this.lname);
}

let myObj2 = new myObj("Jane", "Doe");//This is an object for Jane Doe
```

In this example, we have a function constructor called myObj, which takes two arguments called first and last. We can invoke the myObj function to create a new object with the keyword new and assign this new object to a new variable, which in the example above is called myObj2. Whenever we use this function constructor to build a new object, the *this* keyword will refer to the arguments passed into the function constructor at the time of invocation.

bind, call, and *apply*

We can control where the *this* keyword is pointing using bind, call, and apply. In the example below, we perform function borrowing by using the bind method to invoke a function from within another object. In doing this we create a copy of the first object:

```
let myObj = {
    numberA: 1,
    numberB: 2,
    add: function() {
        return this.numberA + this.numberB;
    }
};

console.log(myObj.add()); //logs 3 i.e. 1 + 2

function newFunc(a, b) {
    let result = this.add();
    return result * a * b;
}

let newObj = newFunc.bind(myObj);
console.log(newObj(3, 4)); //logs 36 i.e. 3 * 3 * 4
```

Instead of making a new object, we can just call the function within the object we want using call or apply. In the case of call we just pass in the object we want *this* to point to as the first argument and then subsequent arguments are regular arguments that we want to pass to that method. In the case of apply, the only difference is that the arguments are supplied as an array list. This allows us to access properties within any object and pass them into a function that is not a method on the object that the properties came from:

```
let myObj = {
    fname: 'jack',
    lname: 'last',
        full: function() {
            return this.fname + ' ' + this.lname;
    }
}

function newFunc(a, b) {
    return "Employee: " + this.fname + ' ' + this.lname + ' ' + a + ' ' + b;
}

console.log(newFunc.apply(myObj, ['address', 'age']));//Employee: jack last address age

console.log(newFunc.call(myObj, 'address', 'age'));//Employee: jack last address age
```

Here is another example that allows us to use call to invoke a method on a nested object while setting this to the outer object:

```
let myObj1 = {
    fname: 'jack',
    lname: 'last',
    myObj2: {
        full: function() {
            return this.fname + ' ' + this.lname;
        }
    }
}

/*
if we invoke the nested method, full, within myObj2
this is pointing the myObj2 which does not contain
fname and lname
*/
console.log(myObj1.myObj2.full());//undefined undefined

/*
we call the method on the nested object i.e. myObj2
but point this to the outer object i.e. myObj1
*/
console.log(myObj1.myObj2.full.call(myObj1));//jack last
```

Assignment 3.3

Extend the *doMath* function displayed in this section under Higher-order functions, to include callbacks that provide an ability to divide two arguments, and converts two floating-point values down to their nearest integer. You can call these functions, myDivider, and myFloater.

Write a JavaScript function that accepts a number as a parameter and checks whether the number is prime or not, and logs the results to the console in each case. (*hint*: a prime number is a whole number greater than 1 whose only factors are 1 and itself, e.g. 2, 3, 5, 7, 11, 13)

Provide a piece of code that uses the apply method and then do the same thing for the bind method.

Conditions and Loops

The JavaScript interpreter will typically go through your code one line at a time until it reaches the end of the code, and in doing so, the JavaScript compiler executes these statements one after another in the order they are written. However, it is possible to design constructs that will only wait until a statement or condition is satisfied before moving to the next step. The result of this construct is that the default behavior for the interpreter is altered until something happens, after which point, the interpreter will continue to execute the remainder of the code line by line. Like all other programming languages, JavaScript has several different ways to code such a construct. These include Conditionals statements, like if and switch, that will wait to check various conditions before proceeding, and Loop statements, like while and for, that run statements repetitively. Here we will examine the various statement and loop structures that JavaScript has to offer.

If statement

The if statement is a fundamental control statement that allows JavaScript to execute a block of code based on a condition. The if statement can have multiple nested conditions and in each case only if a given expression is evaluated will the code inside be executed. The basic syntax of the if statement is as follows:

```
if (person == null) {
    //  do something
}
```

Here, we check to see if the person variable is equal to null, and if it evaluates as true, we will then run the code inside the curly braces. If not we will move onto the code outside the curly braces.

We can also have nested conditions as shown below, where multiple conditions are evaluated and in any case if the condition evaluates to true, the code inside that condition's curly braces will be executed and then the interpreter will break out of the statement

```
let n = 10;

if (n == 1) {
    console.log(n + '= 1');
} else if (n == 2) {
    console.log(n + '= 1');
} else if (n == 3) {
    console.log(n + '= 1');
} else {
    console.log(n + ' is not equal to 1, 2, or 3');// this will be logged
}
```

Switch statement

The switch statement computes the value of an expression and then looks for a case whose expression evaluates to the same value (where same in this case is determined by the === operator). The switch keyword is followed by an expression in parentheses and a block of code in curly braces. When a switch executes, it runs through different cases or conditions to check for evaluation, and if it evaluates will then run the conde inside that case before breaking out of the switch statement altogether. The switch statement also provides a final possibility that will evaluate by default if none of the other cases evaluates to true. However, addition of a default case is optional. The following switch statement is equivalent to the if/else statement shown above:

```
switch (n) {
    case 1:
        n == 1;
        console.log(n + '= 1');
        break;
    case 2:
        n == 2;
        console.log(n + '= 2');
        break;
    case 3:
        n == 3;
        console.log(n + '= 3');
        break;
    default:
        console.log(n + ' is not equal to 1, 2, or 3');
}
```

While Loop

To execute a while loop, the interpreter first evaluates a statement. The while loop will continually loop through a code block until a condition evaluates to false. Here is a simple example of a while loop that logs the value of an outer variable called counter, and will repeatedly do this as long as the value of counter is less than 10. During each loop, the value of counter is incremented by using the syntax, counter++, which is shorthand for counter = counter + 1:

```
var counter = 0;
while (counter < 10) {
    console.log(counter);
    counter++;
}
```

Do/While Loop

The do/while loop is very similar to the While loop that we just examined, with the one exception being the position of condition. In a do/while loop the top of the loop is always going to be executed at least once. It will then evaluate an expression after the first iteration of the loop and if the condition is true, it will do another iteration, and repeat this logic until the expression evaluates to false. In the example below, we set a variable, myNum to the value 5. We then log the value of 5 to the console, and increment the value using the myNum++ syntax. Next is the condition, which asks if myNum is less than 10, and if this evaluates to true, will repeat the do part of the loop and log the new value to the console and again increment the value of myNum. This will result in the numbers 5, 6, 7, 8, and 9 being logged to the console. Once 9 is logged, it will increment and then become 10, thus evaluating the expression to false and breaking out from the do/while loop:

```
let myNum = 5;
do {
    console.log(myNum + ' ');
    myNum++;
} while (myNum < 10);
// 5 6 7 8 9
```

For Loop

For Loops are a much more common looping structure in JavaScript. The For loop defines an index and sets the upper limit of the index, and then executes a piece of code until that upper limit is reached. In the example below, we have defined an array called people composed of 4 elements. Using the keyword for, we define the limit of the loop as zero up to the length of the array which is determined using the length property (remember arrays are objects!), and each time we will increment the index which we define as i. In each step of the loop, we log the array element to the console as follows:

```
let people = ["bob", "jim", "sarah", "mary"];
let i;
for (i = 0; i < people.length; i++) {
    console.log(people[i]);//logs each entry in the array
}
```

For/in Loop

The for/in loop is another very common loop structure in JavaScript which is used to loop through objects. In the example below, we define an object called people, which contains three properties that are each composed of one name value pair. Similarly to the For loop in the previous example, we next declare an index called i, and then set the expression, for i in people, using the keywords *for* and *in*. The meaning of this is that for each property within the people object the code inside the curly braces will be executed once. In this case, the code inside the curly braces will log the property value for each property in the people object to the console. Once we reach the end of the object, the interpreter will break out of the for/in loop:

```
let people = { fname: "Jane", lname: "Doe", age: 38 };


let i;
for (i in people) {
    console.log(people[i]); //logs each property value in object
}
```

Labelled Statements

Statements can be labelled by providing a label at the start of a statement followed by a colon. You can then set up a for loop for example, that contains an if statement condition followed by the keyword *continue* and the label you provided. If the statement inside the if condition evaluates to true the code below the if statement will be executed, and if the statement evaluates to false the code below the if statement will be skipped, and the outer condition will be tested, which is structured as a for loop statement. As an example, below we label our statement evalOdd. The for loop sets a variable called i to 0, and then checks whether it is an odd number. If it is odd, it will continue and execute the code below the *continue* evalOdd statement. If it is not an odd number, then it will go back to the for loop and increment and check the condition again, and repeat this behavior until the upper limit defined in the for loop (where i < 10) is reached, at which point the interpreter will break out from the labelled statement all together:

```
evalOdd:
for (let i = 0; i < 10; i++) {
    if (i % 2 != 1) continue evalOdd;
    console.log(i);
    //1, 3, 5, 7, 9
}
```

It is important to note that you can name a label the same name as a function or other variable, as their namespaces are insulated, however, it cannot be named a reserved keyword.

Assignment 3.4

Write a function that uses a for loop to take an integer argument and return the factorial for that number. For example, it may take the number 4 and then calculate 4 * 3 * 2 * 1 = 24.

Write a JavaScript for loop that will iterate from 0 to 15. For each iteration, it will check if the current number is odd or even, and display a message to the screen declaring whether it is even or odd

Use Strict

The *use strict* feature was introduced in ECMAScript version 5. It is not a statement, but a literal string expression. The purpose of adding the "use strict" string is to indicate that the code should be executed under a strict mode. With strict mode, you cannot have any undeclared variables in your code, and avoiding undeclared variables is often very helpful in avoiding bugs or namespace collisions. Strict mode can also be declared to a function by adding use strict; to the beginning of the function. However, declaring it at the beginning of a script will provide a global scope, meaning that all code in the script will be executed in the strict mode. The syntax for applying use strict is as follows:

```
"use strict";
myVar = 'hello'; // error because myVar is not declared
```

Pattern Matching

In JavaScript when you want to know whether a pattern is found in a string, you can use the test or search methods. Test will return a Boolean type value i.e. true or false if the match is found:

```
let myString = "JavaScript Rocks";
let myPattern = new RegExp("ocks");
let myResult = myPattern.test(myString);
console.log(myResult);//true
```

If you use the search method, it will return the position of the match as follows:

```
let myString = "JavaScript Rocks";
let myPattern = "ocks";
let myResult = myString.search(myPattern);
console.log(myResult);//12
```

Note, that in the search pattern example above, the index for the string starts at zero and white spaces are included as indexed characters.

There are also meta characters that can be used to find certain types of matches, for example only numbers or only letters, or matches at certain positions. Here is a list of the main meta search characters:

Meta Character	Description
.	Find any single character, except newline or end of line character
\w	Find a word character
\W	Find a non word character
\d	Find a digit
\D	Find a non digit character
\s	Find a whitespace character
\S	Find a non whitespace character
\b	Find a match at the beginning/end of a word
\B	Find a match not at the beginning/end of a word
\n	Find a new line character
\r	Find a carriage return character
\t	Find a tab character
^	Beginning of input
$	End of input

As an example of how to use these meta character in your code, the following example searches for a pattern, Ja, that only occurs as the start of a string by using the ^ meta character as follows:

```javascript
let myString = "JavaScript Rocks";
let myPattern = myString.search(/^Ja/);
console.log(myPattern); //0 ---> index of match
```

Accessing the DOM with JavaScript

Similarly to the way you can access DOM elements with CSS, you can also access the DOM using JavaScript. Using JavaScript, you can access the DOM to find HTML elements by id, tag name, class name, CSS selectors, and by HTML object collections. In the example below, we use JavaScript to access the HTML element with the id='myFirstId' by using the getElementById method on the global document object. This will return the entire element, which is not what we want, instead we want to access the text between the tags and to do this we use the innerHTML method as follows:

```html
<h1 id='myFirstId'>hello world</h1>

<script>

let myEl = document.getElementById('myFirstId');
console.log(myEl);//<h1 id="myFirstId">
let myId = document.getElementById('myFirstId').innerHTML;
console.log(myId);//hello world

</script>
```

The innerHTML method can also be used to modify the text between tags as follows:

```html
<h1 id='myFirstId' onclick="myFunction();">hello world</h1>
<script>

function myFunction() {
    /* we can change the text between the tags
    using the innerHTML method*/
    document.getElementById('myFirstId').innerHTML = "hello universe";
}

</script>
```

To access a DOM element by tag you can use the getElementsByTagName method. Note: the plural on Elements. This will return a HTML collection of all specified tags. Individual tags can be accessed numerically (starting at index 0) based on when they appear on the page. In the following example, we capture all 3 header <h1> tags and then print out their corresponding innerHTML based on their sequence i.e. 0 corresponds to the first <h1> and 1 corresponds to the next one:

```
<h1>hello world 1</h1>
<h1>hello world 2</h1>
<h1>hello world 3</h1>

<script>
let myTag = document.getElementsByTagName('h1');
console.log(myTag[0].innerHTML); //hello world 1
console.log(myTag[1].innerHTML); //hello world 2
console.log(myTag[2].innerHTML); //hello world 3
</script>
```

To access a DOM tag within another tag you can assign the outer tag with an ID and then get the tag from the outer ID element that is returned. In the example below, we assign the outer div tag with a unique ID (all IDs must be unique) and then use the variable assigned to this ID to access the inner tags as follows:

```
<div id="outer">
    <p>P tag header</p>
    <h1>h1 tag header</h1>
</div>

<script>
let myOuterTag = document.getElementById('outer');
let myInnerTag = myOuterTag.getElementsByTagName('p');
let myOtherInnerTag = myOuterTag.getElementsByTagName('h1');
console.log(myInnerTag[0].innerHTML); //P tag header
console.log(myOtherInnerTag[0].innerHTML); //h1 tag header
```

You can also access elements by class by assigning tags with class names. Remember that only ID needs to be unique. You can then access the individual class elements based on their index as follows:

```
<p class="myFirstClassTag">P tag header 1</p>
<p class="myFirstClassTag">P tag header 2</p>

<script>
let myClassTag = document.getElementsByClassName('myFirstClassTag');
console.log(myClassTag[0].innerHTML); //P tag header 1
console.log(myClassTag[1].innerHTML); //P tag header 2
</script>
```

You can also use CSS query selectors to access DOM elements by using the querySelectorAll method as follows:

```
<p class="myFirstClassTag">P tag header 1</p>
<p class="myFirstClassTag">P tag header 2</p>

<script>
let myClassTag = document.querySelectorAll('p.myFirstClassTag');
console.log(myClassTag[0].innerHTML); //P tag header 1
console.log(myClassTag[1].innerHTML); //P tag header 2
</script>
```

When it comes to accessing forms, you can also use ID and classes to mark form fields and access them using the syntax shown above. In the following example, you have a simple form with two fields for first name and last name. Whatever value is entered into a field, it can be accessed by using the .value method as follows:

```
<form id="myForm" action="/action_page.php">
    First Name: <input type="text" id="firstName" value="Jane"><br>
    Last Name: <input type="text" id="lastName" value="Doe"><br><br>
    <input type="submit" value="Submit">
</form>

<script>
    let fName = document.getElementById('firstName');
    console.log(fName);//<input id="firstName" value="Jane" type="text">
    console.log(fName.value);//Jane
</script>
```

An alternative approach is to grab the entire form using the document.forms method and access individual values based on their index as follows:

```
<form id="myForm" action="/action_page.php">
    First Name: <input type="text" class="firstName" value="Jane"><br>
    Last Name: <input type="text" id="lastName" value="Doe"><br><br>
    <input type="submit" value="Submit">
</form>

<script>
    let fName = document.forms['myForm'];
    console.log(fName[0].value);//Jane
    console.log(fName[1].value);//Doe
    console.log(fName[2].value);//Submit
</script>
```

It is also possible to use tag names to collect items and in the case of select items, you can set the select tag to a specific id and then obtain the value for that id as follows:

```
<form id="myForm"  >
    First Name:
    <input type="text" class="firstName" value="Jane">
    <br> Last Name:
    <input type="text" id="lastName" value="Doe">
    <br>
    <select name="country" id="makeSelection">
        <option value="USA" id='us'>USA</option>
        <option value="Japan" id='jp'>Japan</option>
        <option value="China" id='cn'>China</option>
        <option value="France" id='fr'>France</option>
    </select>
    <input type="submit" value="Submit" onClick="myFunction()">
</form>
<script>
let selectCountry = document.getElementById('us');
console.log(selectCountry); //<option id="us" value="USA">
console.log(selectCountry.value); //USA
let selectCountryAlt = document.getElementsByTagName('select');
console.log(selectCountryAlt); //HTMLCollection [ select ]
console.log(selectCountryAlt[0].value); //USA
/*
this is the most useful example
as it will return the selcted item
*/
function myFunction() {
    let selectItem = document.getElementById('makeSelection');
    alert(selectItem.value); //whatever item is selected
}
```

Assignment 3.5

Using the form you developed in Section 1, now use JavaScript to get the value from each element and write all the values to the screen once the submit button has been clicked.

Note: you use must include the following methods: getElementById, getElementByTagName, getElementByClassName, and querySelector

PART 4: MAKING APPS WITH HTML, CSS, and JavaScript

Introduction to PhoneGap and Apache Cordova

PhoneGap is a mobile application development framework offered through Adobe Systems. The open source version of the software is called Apache Cordova. Apache Cordova enables software programmers to build applications for mobile devices using CSS, HTML, and JavaScript instead of relying on platform-specific APIs like those in Android, iOS, or Windows Phones. It enables the wrapping of CSS, HTML, and JavaScript code to generate a hybrid mobile application that is not fully native nor fully web based as it becomes wrapped in a platform specific model. The resulting layout rendering is done via web views instead of the platform's native UI framework. The main advantage of using Apache Cordova is that you only need to write your code once in order to deploy it across multiple platforms. Furthermore, there is a very diverse ecosystem of tools available for developers to make the task of developing apps very straightforward while offering comprehensive frameworks and libraries to facilitate diverse mobile application features and functionalities.

Becoming an Android and iPhone app developer

In order to deploy iPhone or Android apps you first need to become an Apple developer or a Google App Developer. Becoming an Apple app Developer is very straightforward. However, it is important to note that you do need a Mac computer or laptop in order to develop iPhone apps. This is because you will need a Mac to generate a signed certificate, which we will cover later in this section. To become a Google Android app developer you can do this using a PC or Mac. To become an Apple developer, first visit the following URL:

Figure 4. Website to enroll in Apple Developer Program

At this site, you can follow their instructions to set up an account as an individual or an organization. You just click the enroll button at the bottom of the page and create an account.

What You Need To Enroll

Enrolling as an Individual

If you are an individual or sole proprietor/single person business, sign in with your Apple ID to get started. You'll need to provide basic personal information, including your legal name and address.

Figure 5. Apple Developer Enrollment Process

Once you created your account, you can then pay for membership, which is $99 per year for individuals and $299 per year for organizations. However, you only need to pay this when you are ready to launch your app in the iTunes app store and so waiting until you are ready will maximum your membership time line. Once you are a member you can generate certificates and profiles for your app.

To become a Google App Developer, you will need a Google email account (if you do not have one, do not worry – it is free! see here www.gmail.com). Once you have an account you can visit the Google Play Developer site at the following URL:

Figure 6. Google Play Developer Site.

You will be asked which type of account you would like to log in using; just select the Gmail account you want to use for your developer account and then register. Once you enroll, you will be asked to pay $25 for membership (one-time fee). You can then launch the Google Play console and start uploading your apps for deployment.

Figure 7. Google Play Console

Installing Apache Cordova

In order to install Apache Cordova you will need to download Node and the Node Package Manager (called npm). They are both bundled together with the latest Node download and so you only really need to download Node from the following website - https://nodejs.org/en/download/:

Figure 8. Website to download Node and npm

Node is an open-source, cross-platform JavaScript run-time environment that executes JavaScript code server-side. The npm tool is a package manager for the JavaScript programming language. The npm package manger is the default package manager for the JavaScript runtime environment Node. It consists of a command line client, also called npm, and an online database of packages, called the npm registry. The registry is accessed via the client, and the available packages can be browsed and searched via the npm website - https://www.npmjs.com/:

Figure 9. Node Packager Manger Website

Once you have installed Node and npm, you can check that they are installed correctly by opening the terminal on a Mac and typing node -v and npm -v. This should return the version numbers as shown below if everything was installed correctly. On a PC, you can open a command window and enter the same commands:

```
$ node -v
```

```
$ npm -v
```

Figure 10. Check installation with these commands

If you are unsure how to open a terminal on a Mac, you can open the finder and just search terminal and double click on the terminal icon or open finder and enter the Applications folder and then enter the Utilities folder and double click on the terminal icon within the Utilities folder. On a PC, you can type Win (i.e. Windows key) + R and then type cmd followed by the return key on your keyboard to open the window cmd prompt.

Once you have confirmed that both Node and npm are correctly installed, you can simply type the following command to install Apache Cordova:

```
$ npm install -g cordova
```

Figure 11. Command to install Cordova

Running Apache Cordova

Once Cordova is installed correctly (Note: use cordova -v command to check correct installation) it is very easy to use Cordova Apache to generate an app template using the following command:

```
$ phonegap create myApp
```

Figure 12. Command to install app template

This will generate a directory called myApp, which you can open and navigate. You will see the directories and sub-directories shown below (Figure 13). The most important of these for now is the /www folder which contains the code that will be used to build platform specific apps. You can open these files and edit them or just remove the files within the /www folder and replace them with your own HTML, CSS, and JavaScript files for you own application.

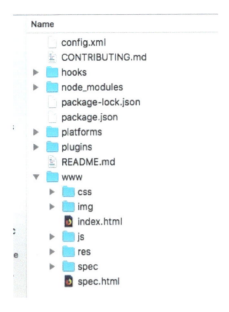

Figure 13. Directory structure for template app

Another important file within the template app that Cordova has generated it the config.xml file which contains information such as the name, description etc. for your app and the relative paths to all the icons that your application will use for different platforms (i.e. iPhone or Android). These icon images are contained within the /res folder within the /www directory (see Figure 13). There are numerous online icon generators, that will generate all (or most) of the icons that you will need for iPhone or Android apps. For Android apps, the following generator works very well for most of the icons:

- https://romannurik.github.io/AndroidAssetStudio/index.html

For iPhone apps, the following generator can be used for most icons:

- https://makeappicon.com/

Place these icons in your own /res folder within the /www folder and manually fix the file paths within the config.xml file. You may also notice a folder called /platforms, which is empty for now, but we will populate this folder later in the section below called Adding Device Specific Platforms, however, before we do this we have to install the Java SDK and Android Studio software in order to create Android specific platforms.

Testing your app

After designing your app in the /www folder of your Cordova template, you can test it in the browser. In Chrome and Firefox you can open the developer tools console (as described in the Debugging Tools section in Section 3 of this book) and click the icon that looks like a mobile phone (Figure 14, bottom right red circle) to view what the site would look like on a mobile phone or specific device:

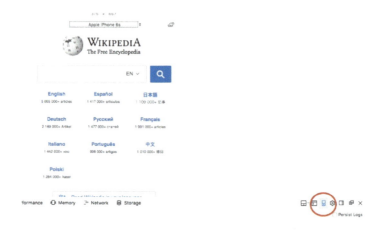

Figure 14. Mobile Phone rendering of site

You can also change the rendering platform based on screen size or device type. In Figure 14, it shows the site rendering for Wikipedia on a mobile phone by using the Firefox developer tools console. Another great option for testing your mobile app on an Android device is to use the PhoneGap Android app. You can download it for free if you have an Android device at the following page:

- https://play.google.com/store/apps/details?id=com.adobe.phonegap.app&hl=en_US

This is a great way to test various features in your designed app. To use the PhoneGap app, you can open a terminal (on Mac) or command window (PC) and move into the folder containing your app on your computer. You can use the cd command to move into a folder and use the ls (or dir command on PC) command to see the contents of where you are currently located. You can then type the following command - phonegap serve - as shown in Figure 15 below. This returns an IP address that you can type into your PhoneGap app on your Android device to test its functionality on an Android device:

```
Damiens-Air:Neurocalc dmohalloran$ phonegap serve
[phonegap] starting app server...
[phonegap] listening on 192.168.1.170:3000
[phonegap]
[phonegap] ctrl-c to stop the server
[phonegap]
```

Figure 15. Using the PhoneGap app

Adding device specific platforms

Once you are happy with how your app looks and feels after testing, you are then ready to add device specific platforms. To add the iPhone platform (i.e., iOS) to your app, you do not need to download any specific software. You can add the ios platform to your app as follows just by moving into the directory e.g. cd myApp and then typing the following command:

$ cordova platform add ios

Figure 16. Command to add iOS platform

In order to do this for the Android platform, Cordova will search for a version of Android Studio on your computer that requires the Java JDK. Therefore, you will need to install both of these tools first on your system (both free). You can download this software at the following sites:

- https://developer.android.com/studio/install

- http://www.oracle.com/technetwork/java/javase/downloads/index.html

Once these are installed, you can then type the following command to install the android platform:

$ cordova platform add android

Figure 17. Install the android platform to your app

You will now notice that the platform directory within your app (see Figure 13) contains the iOS and android platforms. Note: On a PC, you may need to have the Android Studio open when you run the command in Figure 17.

97

Keys and Certificates

Android

Android requires that all Application Package Kits (APKs) be digitally signed with a certificate before they can be installed. A public-key certificate, also known as a digital certificate or an identity certificate, contains the public key of a public/private key pair, as well as some other metadata identifying the owner of the key (for example, name and location). The owner of the certificate holds the corresponding private key. When you sign an APK, the signing tool attaches the public-key certificate to the APK. The public-key certificate serves as a fingerprint that uniquely associates the APK to you and your corresponding private key. This helps Android ensure that any future updates to your APK are authentic and come from you alone. The key used to create this certificate is called the app signing key. Every app must use the same certificate throughout its lifespan in order for users to be able to install new versions or updates to the app. To generate the key, you can use the keytool from Oracle, which can be downloaded from here:

- https://docs.oracle.com/javase/6/docs/technotes/tools/windo ws/keytool.html

All you need to do is cd into your app folder and type the following (for an app called myApp):

Keytool -genkey -v -keystore [location of your app].keystore -alias [yourAppName]Alias -keyalg RSA -keysize -2048 -validity 10000

This will generate a 2,048 bit RSA key pair and self-signed certificate (SHA256 with RSA) with a validity of 10,000 days. You will be asked to insert some details that include a password for your certificate. You will then upload this to PhoneGap Build, which is covered in the next section. Note: in order to execute the keytool command, you will need the Java JDK installed, which was covered in the previous section.

iPhone

For iPhone app development, you will need a Mac computer or laptop. You will need a Mac for signing and for deployment. For signing you will need two documents: 1) Certificate Signing Request, and 2) Provisioning Profile. First login to your Apple developer account (from this point forward you will need to have paid $99 to become an Apple Developer). You will see the following screen:

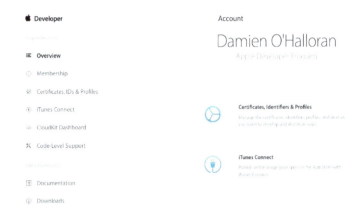

Figure 18. Apple Developer Account Homepage

From here, you can click Certificates, IDs & Profiles from the left menu. You will then be brought to the screen below:

Figure 19. Certificates, Identifiers and Profiles page

From here you can click the + sign in the top right (Figure 19) to create a new certificate. Next, you will open the Utilities Folder on your Mac and open the Keychain Access program as shown in Figure 20:

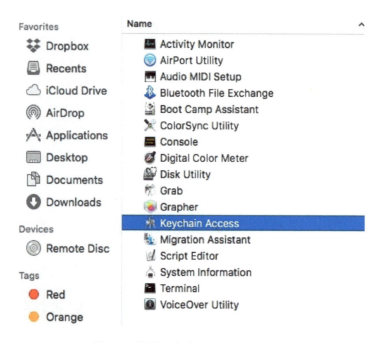

Figure 20. Keychain Access Program

Once you open the Keychain Access tool, you can select the "Request a Certificate from a Certificate Authority" as follows:

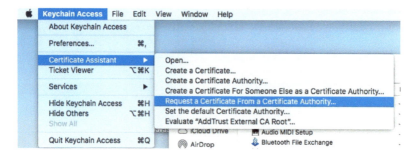

Figure 21. Create a Certificate

You will now enter some details to represent your certificate and then save it to disk in a location such as the Desktop. Now you can go back into your browser and upload the Certificate to your Apple Developer console, and then you can download the validated certificate from your Apple Developer account and open it on your Mac; it will automatically be opened in your Keychain Access program where it will be saved.

Next, you can go back to the Certificates, Identifiers and Profiles page (Figure 19) and at the bottom of the left-hand menu, you can select Provisioning profiles. Similarly for the Certificate above, you can now click the + sign in the top right corner to generate a new Provisioning Profile and follow the instructions to set-up a provisioning profile for distribution on the iTunes app store. Again, you will also download this profile to your desktop.

Note: You will need the Certificate Signing Request and Provisioning Profile to generate an iOS iPhone Application Archive (IPA) build. Similarly, you will need the Digital Certification Key to generate an APK build for Android. We will cover what to do with these Keys and Certs in the next section below.

PhoneGap Build

The next step in preparing your app for deployment is to use the Adobe PhoneGap build site to bundle your app into an APK (Application Package Kit) file for Google Play and an IPA (iPhone Application archive) file for iTunes. First, compress your app into a zip file by selecting your app folder and right clicking on a PC and choose send to myApp.zip. On a Mac you can right-click (or ctrl + click) and choose compress; this will compress your app into a zip file. Next, you can visit the PhoneGap Build site shown below and create a free account at the following webpage:

- https://build.phonegap.com

Figure 22. PhoneGap Build website

Once you have created an account on PhoneGap build, and uploaded your file you can click on the iOS or Android icon and build your app for each platform. You will also be asked to upload the Certificate Signing Request and Provisioning Profile for the iOS build, or the Certificate key for Android builds that we covered in the previous section. Note: it is very important to remember the passwords associated with your keys, as you will be asked for it each time you update and rebuild your app. In Figure 23 below, we show a sample of what the PhoneGap build page looks like.

Figure 23. The app interface on PhoneGap Build

Once your app is built for iOS and Android you can download the IPA file (iTunes) and APK file (Google) to move to deployment, which we will cover in the next section below.

Launching your app

Google Play Store

Launching your app to the Google Play Store is very straightforward. You now have built an APK file in the previous section that you can upload to your Google Play Developer Console. Once you log into your Google Play Developer account, you can click Launch Console, and from there you can select Create Application as shown in Figure 24. You will be required to complete some information about your app including the Content Rating and Pricing. Once you complete these tasks, your app will go live – Congratulations!

Figure 24. Launch App from within the Google Play Console

iTunes App Store

Once you have downloaded the IPA file from PhoneGap Build as discussed previously, you are now ready to launch your app in the iTunes app store, however, before doing that there are a couple of steps you must do. Firstly, you can log into iTunes Connect at the following site:

- https://itunesconnect.apple.com/login

Here you can populate the basic information for your app. When you log in you will see a screen similar to that shown in Figure 25 below:

Figure 25. iTunes Connect Interface

Next, you can click on the tab on the left menu under IOS APP that states Prepare for Submission to declare the version. This is important as when you push your IPA to iTunes Connect it will be waiting for that specific version to sync up correctly. In this view, you will also see a link to download the software called Application Loader (see orange arrow, Figure 26):

Figure 26. Download Application Loader

Once you download the Application Loader tool, you can open it and upload the IPA file that was built using PhoneGap build. The interface for Application Loader is very intuitive and easy to follow:

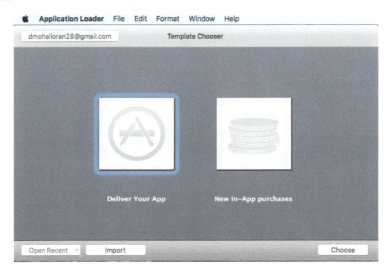

Figure 27. Interface for Application Loader

Once you successfully upload your IPA file using the Application Loader tool, the build will be waiting to approve from within iTunes Connect:

Figure 28. Approve Build from within iTunes Connect

It can take some time (maybe a few hours) before your IPA file appears in your iTunes Connect account, and once it does you can complete some final questions and then launch your app into the iTunes App Store – Congratulations!

About the Author

Damien M. O'Halloran is an Associate Professor in the Department of Biological Sciences at The George Washington University in Washington DC. He teaches courses on Neurobiology and conducts research on neural development and behavior. Dr. O'Halloran's research involves using various bioinformatics and computational approaches that employ JavaScript, Node.js, Perl, MySQL, and HTML5/CSS3; he also develops mobile applications for use in his courses.

www.ingramcontent.com/pod-product-compliance
Lightning Source LLC
Chambersburg PA
CBHW041154050326
40690CB00004B/563